· TROPHIES ·

Intervention
PRACTICE BOOK
Grade 4

Harcourt

Orlando   Boston   Dallas   Chicago   San Diego

Visit *The Learning Site!*
www.harcourtschool.com

Printed in the United States of America

ISBN 0-15-326152-8

3 4 5 6 7 8 9 10 054 10 09 08 07 06 05 04 03 02

Table of Contents

Fluency Builder

anxious	look	land
retire	plant	back
vacant	take	pass
sprucing	stand	spade
adore	see	amazed
recognizing	says	name
	what	gaze

1. This vacant lot / could use / some sprucing up.

2. My gram says / the name / of this flower.

3. I use / a spade / to plant / flowers and bulbs.

4. I am anxious to see / the beautiful flowers / grow.

5. Recognizing / different flowers / can be fun.

6. Take a look / at how pretty / the land looks now.

7. People pass by / just to gaze / at the pretty flowers.

8. They stand back / and adore / the flowers.

9. They are amazed / at what / they see!

Gram's Plant Parade

Read the story. Circle all the words with the short *a* vowel sound. Then draw a line under all the words with the long *a* vowel sound.

Pam has a crate of canned hams. She likes ham with yams. In fact, now she craves some yams to go with her hams. She asks her dad for some. "We are all out, Pam. I will ask Wade if he has yams on his land."

Wade has yams but no ham. Wade will trade some yams for a can of ham. He gets some fat yams out with the blade of his spade. Dad gets a ham. Then Dad and Wade make the trade.

Dad takes the yams to Pam. She bakes the yams in a pan. She gets out some plates. Wade comes over and has some with her and her dad.

Now write the words with a short *a* or a long *a* vowel sound that best complete each sentence.

1. Pam likes to have _____yams_____ with her ham.

2. Her _____dad_____ asks Wade for yams.

3. Wade gets the yams out with his _____spade_____.

4. Pam's dad _____trades_____ a can of ham for some of the yams.

5. Pam _____bakes_____ the yams and ham.

6. _____Wade_____ comes over to have yams and ham with Pam.

Name _____

Gram's Plant Parade

Write one sentence in each box below to tell the main points of "Gram's Plant Parade."

Pages 6–7

Main Idea: Gram sees vacant land at the train station.

Pages 8–9

Main Idea: Gram plants lots of bulbs on the vacant land.

Pages 10–11

Main Idea: At last, Gram's bulbs sprout and the corner looks spruced up.

Now write a one-sentence summary about the story. Use the information from the boxes above.

Possible response: Gram loves to plant, and she spruces up the train station on the corner.

Harcourt

Narrative Elements

Read the paragraph and identify the narrative elements in the story.

Last summer, Adam and his grandpa went fishing at Blue Lake. Adam had never been fishing before. His grandpa taught him how to put a worm on his hook, throw out his line, and wait patiently for a nibble. Adam waited and waited. Finally, he felt a tug on the end of his pole. With the help of his grandpa, Adam landed his first fish. What an exciting day!

Setting

Blue Lake

Characters

Adam and his grandpa

Plot

Possible response: Adam's grandpa teaches him to fish.

Adam catches his first fish.

Harcourt

Fluency Builder

uneasy	things	smile
disappointment	your	pins
compromise	off	nine
perseverance	see	rides
leisure	hat	bike
chortle	can't	pigs
	when	six

1. Miss Wise / collects pins / in her leisure time.

2. "It is a disappointment / when I do not get / the pin I want," / Miss Wise said / with a chortle.

3. Perseverance is / the solution.

4. Bring a collection / of your favorite things / to class.

5. Tim wears six / of his nine hats.

6. Mike rides off / on his bike / to see Jill's collection.

7. Mike thinks Linda / should compromise / with her neighbors / and collect cats / instead of pigs.

8. Mike was uneasy / about his smile collection.

Harcourt

Click!

Read the sentences below. Circle words with the short *i* vowel sound. Draw a line under words with the long *i* vowel sound. Then follow the directions.

1. Jill and Lin take bikes to the lake. Add Lin's bike to the bike rack.
2. Make a swan that glides on the lake.
3. Lin takes his kite to the lake. Make a line from Lin's hand to the kite.
4. Jill wants to go for a hike. Add a hill in the back for Jill to hike up.
5. Mike skates fast. Make a smile on Mike's face.
6. Make five stripes for Mike's skates.
7. The friends will have a picnic. Make a grill for the picnic.

Harcourt

Name_____

Click!

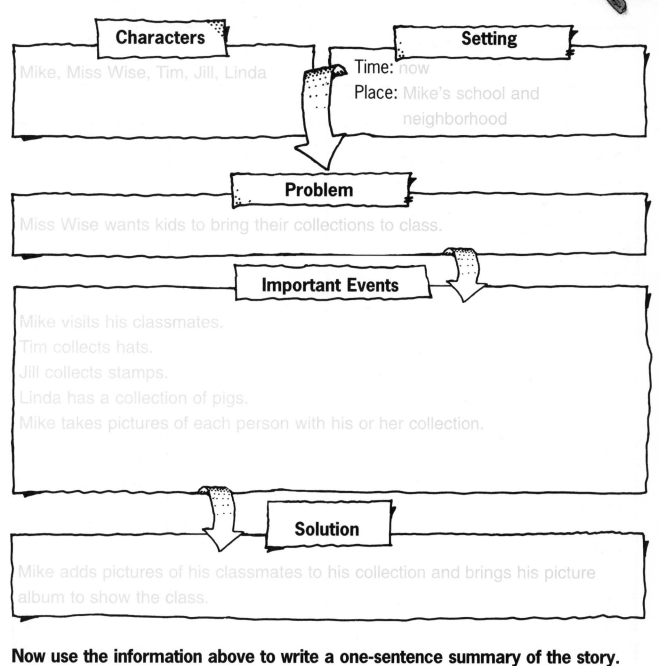

Complete the story map below to summarize the selection.
Be sure to write the events in correct order.

Characters

Mike, Miss Wise, Tim, Jill, Linda

Setting

Time: now

Place: Mike's school and
neighborhood

Problem

Miss Wise wants kids to bring their collections to class.

Important Events

Mike visits his classmates.
Tim collects hats.
Jill collects stamps.
Linda has a collection of pigs.
Mike takes pictures of each person with his or her collection.

Solution

Mike adds pictures of his classmates to his collection and brings his picture
album to show the class.

Now use the information above to write a one-sentence summary of the story.

Possible response: The kids in Miss Wise's class find out that collecting is fun.

Harcourt

Name _____

Prefixes, Suffixes, and Root Words

Read the following words and identify the prefixes, suffixes, and root words.

graceful	preheat	redesign	nonfiction
tenderness	bicycle	improper	uninteresting

Prefixes	Root Words	Suffixes	New Words
	grace	-ful	graceful
pre-	heat		preheat
re-	design		redesign
non-	fiction		nonfiction
	tender	-ness	tenderness
bi-	cycle		bicycle
im-	proper		improper
un-	interesting		uninteresting

Harcourt

Fluency Builder

pageant	class	role
restless	able	fox
tropical	wait	hopes
rehearsals	give	jokes
attentively	nose	nose
troublesome	begin	cope
		flops
		frog

1. Miss Jones's class is planning / a holiday pageant.

2. The pageant is / about a fox, / a dog, / and a frog that visit / a tropical land.

3. Ron hopes / to get the role / of the fox / because it has / the greatest jokes.

4. During dress rehearsals, / Miss Jones gives out the costumes.

5. Everyone waits attentively / to receive his or her costume.

6. Ron's costume / is a troublesome fake fox nose / that flops up and down.

7. Everyone is restless / waiting for the pageant / to begin.

8. Ron is able to cope / with his fake fox nose.

A Troublesome Nose

Write the word that makes the sentence tell about the picture.

1. Robin has a job at Tom's map

_____shop_____ .

hop   **pond**   **shop**

2. At the shop, they have maps and

_____globes_____ .

groves   **globes**   **bones**

3. Tom asks Robin to

_____mop_____ the shop.

mope   **pop**   **mop**

4. The _____pole_____

pole   **mole**   **smoke**

of the mop hits a clock.

5. The clock _____drops_____

robs   **drops**   **tops**

down onto a globe.

6. That's how Robin

_____broke_____

rode   **hop**   **broke**

the clock and the globe.

Harcourt

A Troublesome Nose

Fill in the story map to tell about the main events in "A Troublesome Nose." Use the words in the gray boxes to help you.

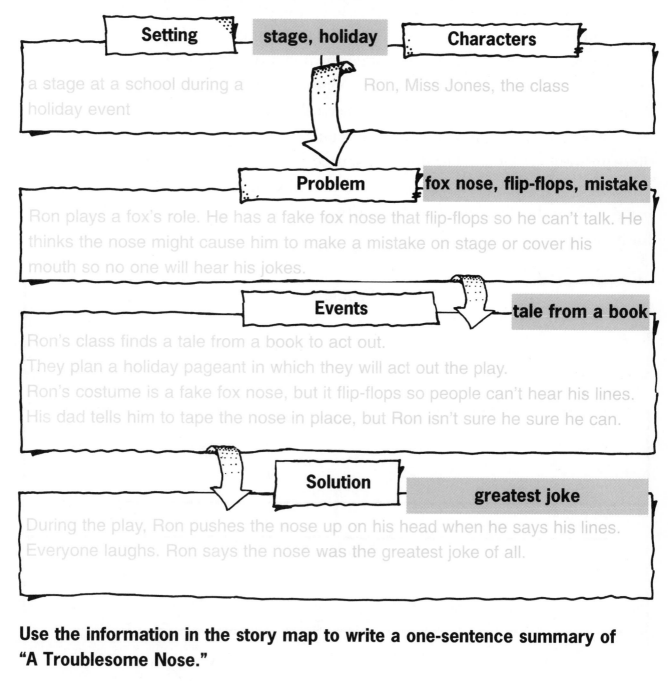

Setting | stage, holiday | Characters

a stage at a school during a holiday event

Ron, Miss Jones, the class

Problem | fox nose, flip-flops, mistake

Ron plays a fox's role. He has a fake fox nose that flip-flops so he can't talk. He thinks the nose might cause him to make a mistake on stage or cover his mouth so no one will hear his jokes.

Events | tale from a book

Ron's class finds a tale from a book to act out.
They plan a holiday pageant in which they will act out the play.
Ron's costume is a fake fox nose, but it flip-flops so people can't hear his lines.
His dad tells him to tape the nose in place, but Ron isn't sure he sure he can.

Solution | greatest joke

During the play, Ron pushes the nose up on his head when he says his lines. Everyone laughs. Ron says the nose was the greatest joke of all.

Use the information in the story map to write a one-sentence summary of "A Troublesome Nose."

Possible response: Ron is a fox in the school play and finds a way to deal

with a troublesome fake nose.

Narrative Elements

Read the paragraph and identify the problem, the problem-solving steps, and the resolution in the story. Possible responses are given.

Daniel walked slowly around the exhibit at the museum. He had never seen a dinosaur skeleton before. Signs all around the museum said Do Not Touch! Daniel knew better than to touch these precious bones. All of a sudden the dinosaur started to move. Daniel turned around and saw that a sleeve of the coat he had tied around his waist was now caught on the dinosaur's tail. He tried to unhook his coat, but the dinosaur wouldn't let go! The dinosaur started to sway even more. Daniel decided to untie the jacket from around his waist. He carefully untied his jacket and left it hanging from the dinosaur's tail. A security guard came by and got Daniel's jacket for him.

Problem:
Daniel's coat gets caught around the dinosaur's tail.

↓

Problem-Solving Steps:
Daniel tries to unhook the coat. Daniel unties the jacket from around his waist and leaves it hanging from the dinosaur's tail.

↓

Resolution:
A security guard gets Daniel's jacket for him.

Harcourt

Fluency Builder

courageous	were	agreed
immigrants	played	team
salary	first	see
tremendous	called	speed
appreciation	find	Yankees
valuable	glad	forget
modest		
sportsmanship		

1. Joe DiMaggio's parents / were immigrants.

2. He played baseball / with a team called / the Yankees.

3. At first / the fans / did not like him, / but Joe / could hit well, / and he had speed.

4. The fans then agreed / that he was a tremendous find.

5. Joe / was valuable / to the team, / and his salary / went up.

6. Baseball fans / will not forget / the courageous sportsmanship / of Joe DiMaggio.

7. He was a modest man, / but he was always glad / to see his fans.

8. He was / voted into / the Baseball Hall of Fame / in appreciation / of all that he gave / to the game.

Harcourt

Name _____

Joe DiMaggio, One of Baseball's Greatest

Fred has a home next to the sea. A seal named Honey comes to see him. Fred feeds Honey a meal of fish. Honey eats. Then Honey dives in and out of some seaweed.

Honey swims down deep to the seabed. Honey sees a net. Honey eats a hole in the net. The fish swim free. Then Honey leaps out of the sea. Fred's feet get wet.

Circle and write the word that best completes each sentence.

1. Fred's home is _____next_____ to the sea.   (**next**)   **bent**   **neat**

2. Fred meets a _____seal_____
named Honey.   **seen**   (**seal**)   **meal**

3. Honey likes to _____eat_____ fish.   (**eat**)   **sweep**   **heat**

4. She dives to the _____seabed_____ .   (**seabed**)   **treetop**   **clean**

5. She sees a _____net_____ .   **heat**   (**net**)   **beam**

6. She _____frees_____ some trapped fish.   (**frees**)   **seats**   **seeds**

7. Then she _____leaps_____ out of the sea.   **gleams**   **weeds**   (**leaps**)

8. Fred gets _____wet_____ .   **ten**   (**wet**)   **wheat**

Joe DiMaggio, One of Baseball's Greatest

These events are from "Joe DiMaggio, One of Baseball's Greatest." They are out of order. Put a number in front of each one to show the right order.

___2___ DiMaggio hit 46 home runs.

___4___ DiMaggio retired.

___1___ DiMaggio made the New York Yankees team.

___3___ DiMaggio did not miss getting a hit in 56 games.

Now write each event from above where it belongs in the story.

DiMaggio made the New York Yankees team.

In 1936 he got 206 hits, and 29 of them were home runs.

His salary went up at the end of the year.

DiMaggio hit 46 home runs.

In 1938 and 1939 he had many hits, but his hitting fell off a little in 1940.

DiMaggio did not miss getting a hit in 56 games.

DiMaggio retired.

In 1955 he was voted into the Baseball Hall of Fame.

He was 84 when his life ended on March 8, 1999.

Prefixes, Suffixes, and Roots

Prefix	Suffix	Root	Meaning
re-			again, back
dis-			not, opposite of
	-less		without
	-ian		person who does
	-ible		able to
		-vis-	see

Write the word that matches each definition. Choose from the words in the box below.

dishonest	visible	dislikes	tasteless	weightless
reuse	redo	replace	musician	politician

1. person who performs music _____ musician _____

2. does not like _____ dislikes _____

3. without weight _____ weightless _____

4. not honest _____ dishonest _____

5. use again _____ reuse _____

6. person in politics _____ politician _____

7. put back _____ replace _____

8. able to be seen _____ visible _____

9. without taste _____ tasteless _____

10. do again _____ redo _____

Harcourt

Fluency Builder

outspoken	quiet	June
practical	asked	fun
brisk	liked	tugged
elegant	with	stuff
elevations	how	stuck
miniatures	what	
starstruck	day	
marveled		

1. Amelia said / it was a starstruck night / outside.

2. Amelia / was outspoken, / but June / was quiet.

3. Amelia liked practical pants, / but June enjoyed elegant dresses.

4. June had fun / with her miniature / tea set.

5. It was / a brisk day / and the fresh breeze / gave her an idea.

6. June marveled / at how brave / Amelia was.

7. Amelia gave June a tape / and asked / "What is / the elevation / of this shed?"

8. She tugged a box / and other stuff / out of the shed.

Name _____

Amelia's Flying Lesson

Circle and write the word that answers each riddle.

1. I have the same vowel sound as in *run*.
   My mom and dad are dogs. What am I?

   _____pup_____

   bug   tube   (pup)

2. I have the same vowel sound as in *rude*.
   You can make a tune with me. What am I?

   _____flute_____

   (flute)   prune   trumpet

3. I have the same vowel sound as in *rut*.
   I rise and set. What am I?

   _____sun_____

   (sun)   tube   tub

4. I have the same vowel sound as in *brute*.
   I am made of sand. What am I?

   _____dune_____

   prune   mud   (dune)

5. I have the same vowel sound as in *hum*.
   You get clean in me. What am I?

   _____tub_____

   rut   (tub)   lube

6. I have the same vowel sound as in *lute*.
   I tell people what to do. What am I?

   _____rule_____

   stub   pollute   (rule)

7. I have the same vowel sound as in *bug*.
   I can be filled with milk. What am I?

   _____cup_____

   cub   (cup)   glue

8. I have the same vowel sound as in *tune*.
   I name a time. What am I?

   _____June_____

   Jules   Jean   (June)

9. I have the same vowel sound as in *bud*.
   You can sweep me up. What am I?

   _____dust_____

   stunt   (dust)   plume

Harcourt

Name _____

Amelia's Flying Lesson

Complete the flowchart with words from the box to tell what happened in "Amelia's Flying Lesson."

climbed	flew	girls
turn	sky	wheels

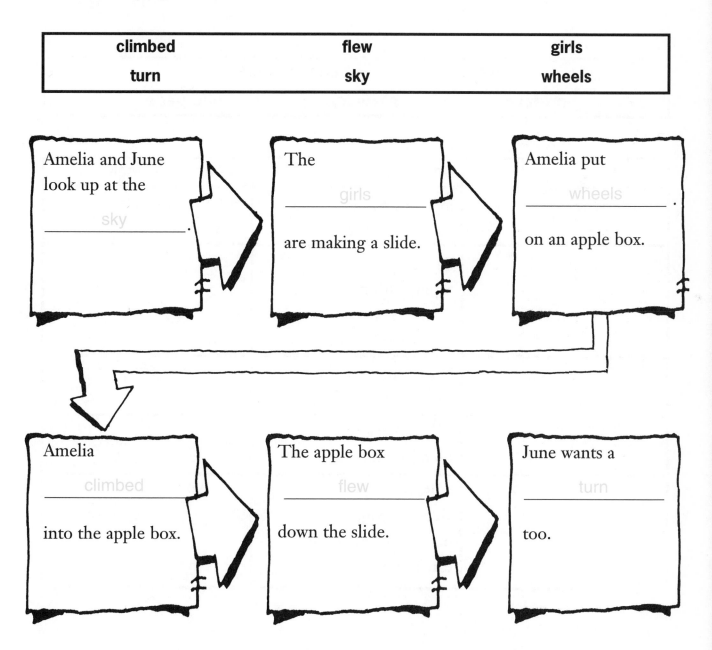

Amelia and June look up at the

_____sky_____ .

The

_____girls_____

are making a slide.

Amelia put

_____wheels_____ .

on an apple box.

Amelia

_____climbed_____

into the apple box.

The apple box

_____flew_____

down the slide.

June wants a

_____turn_____

too.

Now write a one-sentence summary of the story. You may use the flowchart above to help you.

Possible response: Two girls make a slide and go down it on an apple box with wheels.

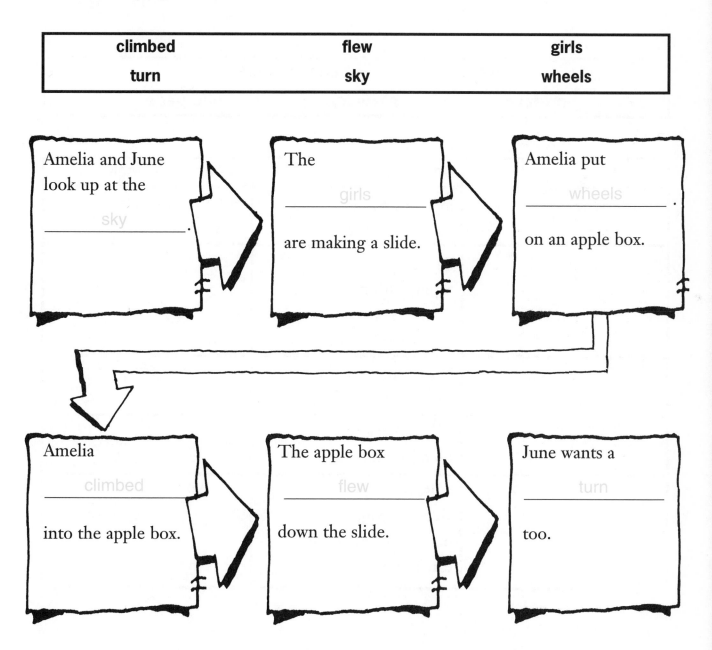 Harcourt

Locate Information

Read the words in the box. Write them in the correct places in the first column. In the third column, tell in which part of a book each is located.

index	table of contents
preface	glossary	title page

Book Part	Description	Location in Book
title page	includes name of book, author, publisher	beginning of book
index	an alphabetical list of topics with page numbers where they can be found	back of the book
preface	a brief introduction to a book	near the front
glossary	a dictionary of terms used in the book	back of the book
table of contents	a list of chapters with the page number where each can be found	front of the book

Harcourt

Fluency Builder

ad lib	began	stall
shiftless	was	Walt
luxury	song	call
privilege	that	all
elated	ask	calmly
shamefacedly	for	already
indignantly		
assent		

1. The CD Man / indignantly said / his business was honest.

2. Walt shamefacedly said / all he had / was five bucks.

3. Walt is not / a shiftless kid; / he is honest.

4. CDs are a luxury, / and you already / have lots / of them.

5. Walt began / to ad lib a song / outside the CD stall.

6. Walt was elated / that the CD Man asked / for the privilege / of selling his songs.

7. Walt calmly nodded his assent / and said he'd bring the songs / next week.

8. "I'd call you / a real can-do kid!" / said the CD Man.

Can-Do Kid

Read the story. Then read each question that follows the story. Circle the letter for the best answer.

It was late in the fall. Jan called Walt. She asked him to go to a baseball game with her. Walt hoped to see a ball hit over a wall. Jan and Walt met on the sidewalk close to the mall. They got on a bus. The bus went to a lot covered with grass that had white lines on it. The baseball game was at the lot.

It was time for the Rams to bat. A tall man walked to the plate with his bat. A small man who played for the Flames tossed him the ball. The batter hit the ball. The ball went over a wall. The Rams got a run. "What a fine hit!" Walt said.

1 Whom did Jan ask to go to the baseball game with her?
 A Walt
 B her dad
 C a tall man on the Rams team

2 When did they go to the game?
 A in the spring
 B in June
 C in the fall

3 What did Walt hope to see?
 A a ball at the mall
 B a ball hit over a wall
 C a small man hit a ball

4 Jan and Walt met _____.
 A in the hall
 B close to the mall
 C at the falls

5 The _____ game was at the lot.
 A ball
 B talk
 C mall

6 With a bat in hand, _____ came to the plate.
 A a bald man
 B Walt
 C a tall man

7 _____ tossed the ball to the plate.
 A A basketball
 B Walt
 C A small man

8 The man on the Rams team hit the ball over a _____.
 A wall
 B mall
 C stall

Can-Do Kid

Name _____

Complete the flowchart with words from the box to tell about "Can-Do Kid."

singing	money	can-do
business	earn	stall

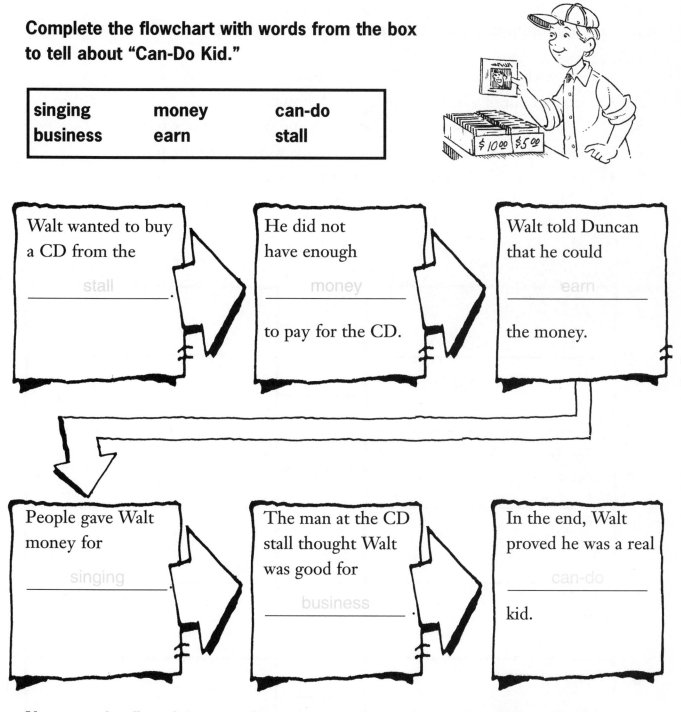

Walt wanted to buy a CD from the

_____stall_____ .

He did not have enough

_____money_____

to pay for the CD.

Walt told Duncan that he could

_____earn_____

the money.

People gave Walt money for

_____singing_____

The man at the CD stall thought Walt was good for

_____business_____ .

In the end, Walt proved he was a real

_____can-do_____

kid.

Now use the flowchart to write a one-sentence summary of the story.

Possible response: A boy proves he can get what he wants if he doesn't give up.

Harcourt

Cause and Effect

Read each sentence. Identify the cause and the effect. Then fill in the boxes.

1. We ate lunch inside because it began to rain.
2. The car ran out of gas, so we had to walk home.
3. We forgot to add a stamp to the envelope, and our letter was returned.
4. My dad fenced in our garden because rabbits were eating the plants.
5. The sun was very hot, and our ice cream melted.
6. I brought my lunch because I didn't like the food that was being served.

	Cause	**Effect** Action
1.	It began to rain.	We ate lunch inside.
2.	The car ran out of gas.	We had to walk home.
3.	We forgot to add a stamp to the envelope.	Our letter was returned.
4.	Rabbits were eating the plants.	My dad fenced in our garden.
5.	The sun was very hot.	Our ice cream melted.
6.	I didn't like the food that was being served.	I brought my lunch.

Fluency Builder

insignificant   out   gray
plotting   rope   began
twined   sign   sailed
steely   off   ran
encircling   down   raiding
loyal   hens   last
neglected
unyielding

1. Ray's dog, / Loyal, had / a heavy gray blanket / to sleep on.

2. Ray twined a rope / with a sign on it / to the gate.

3. Loyal stretched out / on his blanket / and began plotting / how to prove he was brave.

4. Ray neglected to close the gate, / so Loyal sailed out / and was off down the street.

5. A big dog said / that Loyal / was small and insignificant.

6. Loyal trotted / around the pen encircling the hens, / to stop the fox / from raiding the pen.

7. The fox grabbed / Loyal's leg / in his steely grip.

8. Loyal was unyielding, / and at last the fox / ran away.

Name

Small But Brave

Circle and write the word that makes the sentence tell about the picture.

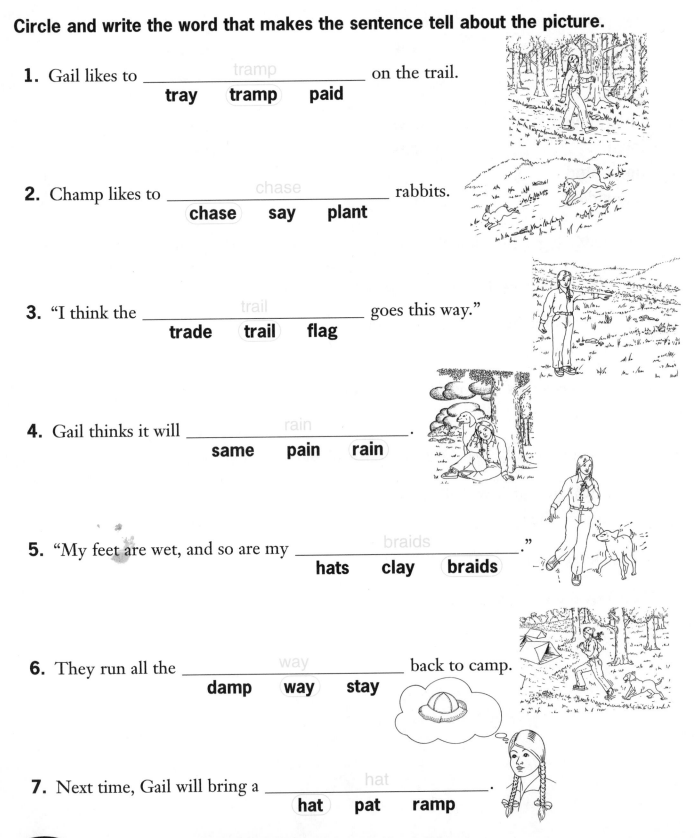

1. Gail likes to _____ tramp _____ on the trail.

    tray   (**tramp**)   **paid**

2. Champ likes to _____ chase _____ rabbits.

    (**chase**)   **say**   **plant**

3. "I think the _____ trail _____ goes this way."

    trade   (**trail**)   **flag**

4. Gail thinks it will _____ rain _____.

    same   **pain**   (**rain**)

5. "My feet are wet, and so are my _____ braids _____."

    hats   **clay**   (**braids**)

6. They run all the _____ way _____ back to camp.

    damp   (**way**)   **stay**

7. Next time, Gail will bring a _____ hat _____.

    (**hat**)   **pat**   **ramp**

Name _____

Small But Brave

Fill in the story map to tell about the main events in "Small But Brave." Use the words in the gray boxes to help you.

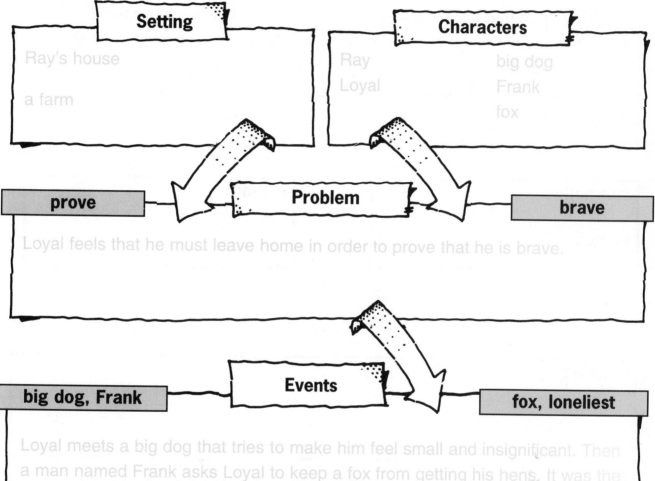

Setting

Ray's house

a farm

Characters

Ray   big dog
Loyal   Frank
             fox

prove

Problem

Loyal feels that he must leave home in order to prove that he is brave.

brave

big dog, Frank

Events

fox, loneliest

Loyal meets a big dog that tries to make him feel small and insignificant. Then a man named Frank asks Loyal to keep a fox from getting his hens. It was the loneliest job of all. After a hard fight with the fox, Loyal decides to go back home to live with Ray.

Now use the information above to write a one-sentence summary to explain the lesson that Loyal learned.

Possible response: Loyal learned that it is more important to have a friend than to prove that you are brave.

Narrative Elements

Read the paragraph and identify the narrative elements in the story. Then fill in the story map.

One day Sarah went to the garage for her bike—but it was not there! Where could it be? She ran to ask her mother for help. Her mother suggested that she think about all the things she had done since yesterday. Sarah remembered riding to the park and leaving her bike near a tree. Then she remembered walking home with her best friend Lisa. That was it! She ran to the park, and sure enough, her bike was exactly where she had left it! Possible responses are given.

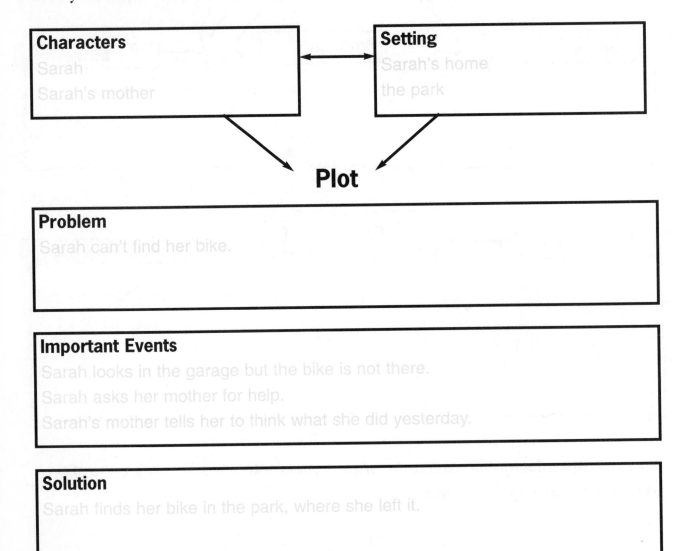

Characters
Sarah
Sarah's mother

Setting
Sarah's home
the park

Plot

Problem
Sarah can't find her bike.

Important Events
Sarah looks in the garage but the bike is not there.
Sarah asks her mother for help.
Sarah's mother tells her to think what she did yesterday.

Solution
Sarah finds her bike in the park, where she left it.

Harcourt

Fluency Builder

uninhabited	come	chicks
burrows	started	rushed
venture	right	fresh
stranded	wanted	fishing
instinctively	years	splashed
nestle	three	with
	again	watches

1. The team / wanted to bring / the puffins back / to the uninhabited / Egg Rock.

2. The team / started with a plan / to bring / the puffins back.

3. A village / of burrows / was made / for the chicks / to nestle in.

4. The team hoped / the puffins / would instinctively return again / in two or three years.

5. The child / watches the puffin / fishing for fresh fish.

6. The children / rushed to help / the young birds that were stranded / in the village.

7. The young birds / splashed into / the water / but did not venture / out any further.

8. Steve Kress / made / the right decision / to come / to Egg Rock.

Bringing Back the Puffins

Read the sentences, and circle the words that have the /sh/, /ch/, or /th/ sound. Then follow the directions.

1. Chen, Seth, and Sasha are having lunch on a ship. Make a dish with chicken for the children.
2. They want some cheese, too. Put a big cheese next to the chicken.
3. Ships have names. Put the name "Marsha" on the side of the ship.
4. The deck of the ship will need to be cleaned. Put a big brush on the deck.
5. Seth sees a shark splashing in the sea. Put a shark in the sea.
6. Chen has a starfish that was on the beach. Put a starfish on the ship's deck.
7. There is a small shed on the deck to put things in. Make a shed on the deck.
8. Sasha will want to fish after lunch. Put a fishing pole next to the shed.
9. Seth made a batch of lemonade. Give each friend a matching glass.

Name _____

Bringing Back the Puffins

These events from "Bringing Back the Puffins" are in the wrong order. Put a number in front of each one to show the correct order.

_____4_____ The chicks left their nests and headed for the sea.

_____2_____ Kress and his team went to a land where puffins lived.

_____3_____ They set up a village of nests for the puffin chicks.

_____1_____ Steve Kress made a plan to bring puffin chicks to Egg Rock.

Now write each event in the order in which it happens in the selection. Put each one next to an X.

X Steve Kress made a plan to bring puffin chicks to Egg Rock.

X Kress and his team went to a land where puffins lived.

They brought puffin chicks back to Egg Rock.

X They set up a village of nests for the puffin chicks.

The team fed the chicks and kept them safe from danger.

X The chicks left their nests and headed for the sea.

Steve Kress watched for the puffins to return to their nests.

Write a one-sentence summary to tell how the story ends.

Possible response: Kress spied a puffin in the sky returning to its home on

Egg Rock.

Harcourt

Summarize

Fill out the first two columns of the K-W-L chart at the bottom of this page. In column 1, write what you know about growing vegetables. In column 2, write what you would like to learn about growing vegetables.

Now read the following paragraph about vegetable gardens.

Growing a vegetable garden requires a great deal of time and energy. In the early spring, the soil must be turned with a shovel or garden hoe. Fertilizer should be added to create a good place for your vegetables to take root. Seeds can be planted as soon as the weather turns warm. Once the seedlings begin to grow, weeds must be pulled out each week and the garden watered often. By late summer, the full-grown vegetables should be picked each day. The garden needs to be cleaned of dead plants in the fall. Delicious vegetables will be the result of all your hard work!

Complete the last column of the chart by summarizing the information you learned from the paragraph.

What I Know	What I Want to Know	What I Learned
You have to follow certain steps to grow a vegetable garden.	What are the steps that have to be followed to grow a vegetable garden.	Growing a vegetable garden takes time and a lot of hard work, but the delicious vegetables that result are worth the effort.

Harcourt

Fluency Builder

haze	bike	carp
inhale	feed	garden
mural	like	harvest
lavender	smell	Marlene
skidded	big	part
	seat	Carla
	from	yard
	wanted	

1. Martin skidded his bike / to a stop, / making a haze of dust.

2. Martin wanted / to feed the carp / in the pond.

3. Miss Marlene likes to inhale / the sweet smells / from the garden / while sitting on the garden seat.

4. Nick measured neat lines / for the next part / of his garden mural.

5. The small green tomatoes were / for the next big harvest.

6. Nick saw a line of lavender petals / leaving the garden.

7. The petals led Nick / to Carla and Lil's yard.

8. Carla did her part / to show Nick / that the green tomatoes / were not useless.

Green Tomatoes

Read the story. Circle all the words with the /är/ sound you hear in *hard*.

Marta and Bart collect marbles. They like the game of marbles a lot. "We could start a marble game in the corner of the yard," says Marta. She and Bart find a spot by the barn. They make a target for the marbles in the dust.

It's hard to hit a target with a marble. Marta and Bart become skilled at it over time. Marta makes some amazing hits with her favorite red marble. Bart likes to flip his marbles hard at the target. Over time, some of the marbles get lost.

Bart and Marta get the greatest marbles at the market down the street. The marbles are in a corner of the market. The friends see beans, peas, and parsnips. Then they see yarn, car wax, and a yardstick. At last they find the marbles next to the greeting cards.

Now write the word with the /är/ sound that best completes each sentence.

1. Marta and _____ Bart _____ collect marbles, and they like marble games.

2. They take their marbles to the corner of the _____ yard _____.

3. They make a _____ target _____ by the barn.

4. Bart flips his marbles _____ hard _____ at the target.

5. Marta and Bart get their marbles at the _____ market _____.

6. They find the marbles next to the greeting _____ cards _____.

Harcourt

Green Tomatoes

Complete the sentences with a word from the box.

petals	season	garden	tomatoes	vines	measured

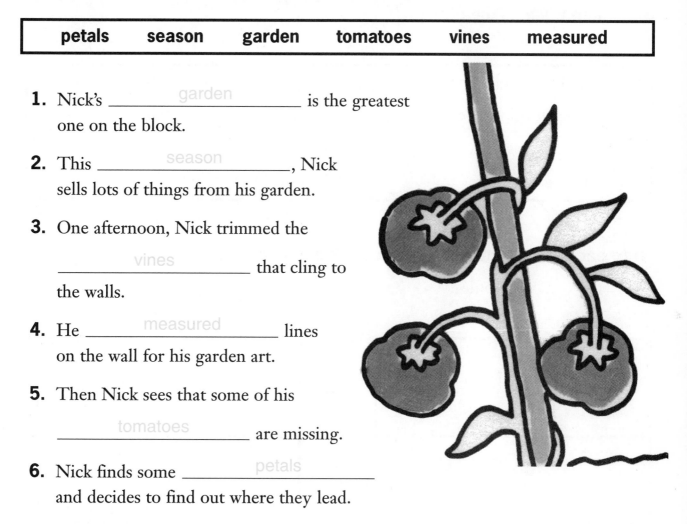

1. Nick's _____garden_____ is the greatest one on the block.

2. This _____season_____, Nick sells lots of things from his garden.

3. One afternoon, Nick trimmed the _____vines_____ that cling to the walls.

4. He _____measured_____ lines on the wall for his garden art.

5. Then Nick sees that some of his _____tomatoes_____ are missing.

6. Nick finds some _____petals_____ and decides to find out where they lead.

Now write two or three sentences to summarize what happens in the rest of the story.

Possible response: The petals lead to Carla and Lil's yard.

Lil is hitting the tomatoes with her bat. Carla and Lil give Nick a jar of

pickled green tomatoes to sell to make up for his missing tomatoes.

Cause and Effect

Read each pair of statements. For each pair, decide which statement is the cause and which is the effect.

There was broken glass everywhere.	The glass bottle fell on the floor.
The thunderstorm was beginning.	Our field trip was cancelled.
The back door was left open.	The cat ran outside.
The baby began to cry.	Alex made a loud noise.

Write each statement in the correct box on the chart.

Cause		**Effect**
The glass bottle fell on the floor.	→	There was broken glass everywhere.
The thunderstorm was beginning.	→	Our field trip was cancelled.
The back door was left open.	→	The cat ran outside.
Alex made a loud noise.	→	The baby began to cry.

Harcourt

Fluency Builder

smuggled	hear	approach
facial	some	coax
displeasure	away	grown
endangered	takes	show
coordination	through	own
jealous	been	roaming
	overgrown	
	noise	

1. Did you hear / that noise? / Roaming / through the trees / is a baby orangutan!

2. A jealous orangutan / uses facial expressions / to show / its displeasure.

3. Do not / approach / a baby orangutan / or try to coax it away / from its mother.

4. The orangutan / is an / endangered animal.

5. Some / have been smuggled / out of the country.

6. It takes a lot / of coordination / to swing / through the overgrown trees.

7. When an orangutan has grown, / it makes / its own nest.

8. The poster / shows a baby orangutan / hugging its mother.

Name _____

A Day with the Orangutans

Read the story. Circle all the words that have the long vowel sound of *o*.

Joan has a white goat named Snow. She takes Snow to show at the fair. Sometimes Joan has to coax Snow to get her to follow.

Snow is getting a bath. She will be clean for the show. Joan soaks her goat in a tub. She has yellow soap to make Snow's coat shine.

The next day, Snow throws up her heels at the show. Joan moans.

Snow wins a medal for the whitest coat. Owning a goat is fun but hard!

Circle and write the word that best completes each sentence.

1. Joan's _____goat_____ is named Snow.   **goat**   **dog**   **crow**

2. She takes Snow to a _____show_____.   **shop**   **show**   **toad**

3. Joan _____soaks_____ Snow in the tub.   **mows**   **socks**   **soaks**

4. The _____yellow_____ soap makes Snow's coat shine.   **toast**   **white**   **yellow**

5. Snow _____throws_____ up her heels.   **throbs**   **goals**   **throws**

6. This makes Joan _____moan_____.   **grow**   **moan**   **man**

7. _____Owning_____ a goat is fun.   **Bowling**   **Getting**   **Owning**

Harcourt

A Day with the Orangutans

Complete the flowchart with words from the box to tell what happened in "A Day with the Orangutans."

| baby | expressions | practice | orphans | behavior | depend | human |

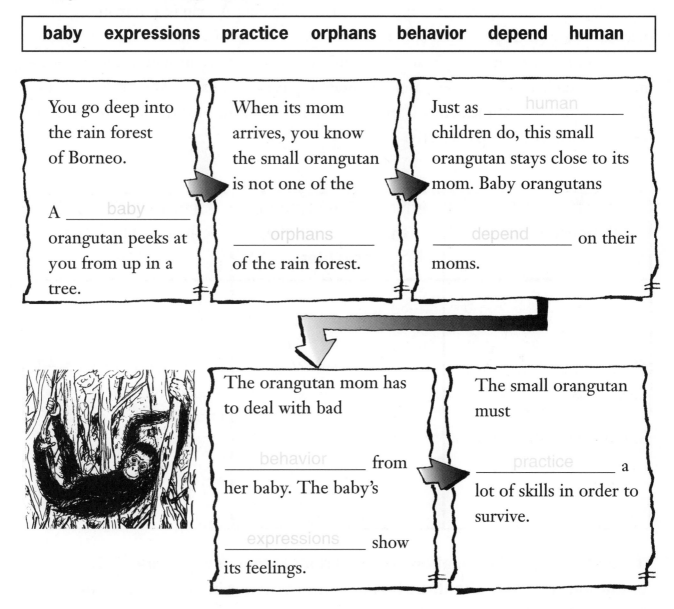

You go deep into the rain forest of Borneo.

A _____baby_____ orangutan peeks at you from up in a tree.

→

When its mom arrives, you know the small orangutan is not one of the

_____orphans_____

of the rain forest.

→

Just as _____human_____ children do, this small orangutan stays close to its mom. Baby orangutans

_____depend_____ on their moms.

The orangutan mom has to deal with bad

_____behavior_____ from her baby. The baby's

_____expressions_____ show its feelings.

→

The small orangutan must

_____practice_____ a lot of skills in order to survive.

Now use the information from the flowchart to write a one-sentence summary of the selection.

Possible response: Orangutan babies depend on their mothers for care and

learn important skills from them.

Harcourt

Summarize

Read the following paragraph, and identify the important information.

Maps show many things about the world we live in. A map is a drawing of a place as you would see it from above. There can be maps of your city, your state, your country, or even your classroom. Symbols are used to represent different things on a map, such as roads, rivers, and mountains. Most maps have a key, or legend, that explains what each of the symbols means. It is important to read the key so you will be able to use your map correctly.

The Most Important Idea	Important Information That Supports the Main Idea	Information That Is Not as Important
Maps are useful, but you need to know how to use the key or legend to use them correctly.	Symbols are used to represent different things on maps. Most maps have keys or legends that explain the symbol's meanings.	A map is a drawing of a place. There can be maps of your city, your state, your country, or even your classroom.

Think about what information you would include in a summary of the paragraph. Which of the three boxes would you not include in a summary? Explain why.

Possible response: The information in the third box does not belong in a

summary, because a summary includes only important information

and main ideas.

Harcourt

Name _____

Fluency Builder

windbreak	**family**	**porch**
rustle	**his**	**more**
alarmed	**down**	**portrait**
paddock	**father**	**roared**
conch	**sea**	**worn**
almost	**in**	**scorched**
fire		**course**

1. Father was alarmed / when he heard / the grass rustle / in the wind.

2. His family / had almost / lost their home / in a grass fire / last summer.

3. From the porch of his house, / he can see the horses / in the paddock.

4. He pictured / how the flames / had roared loudly / as they scorched the roof.

5. Everyone / was worn out / as they put / more and more water / on the fire.

6. His son / had held onto the conch shell / that came / from their old home by the sea.

7. Of course, / Father knows / that the windbreak / now planted around the house / will slow / a fire down.

8. He feels safe / as he looks / at the family portrait / hanging / on the wall.

A Home on the Oregon Trail

Write the word that answers each riddle. Each answer contains the same sound as the _or_ in _for_, but it may be spelled differently.

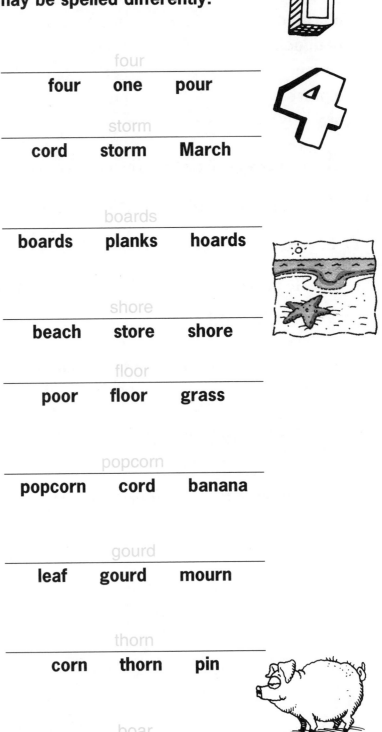

1. My _or_ sound is spelled _our_.
I am a number. What am I? _____ four _____

four	one	pour

2. My _or_ sound is spelled _or_.
I bring wind and rain. What am I? _____ storm _____

cord	storm	March

3. Our _or_ sound is spelled _oar_.
We are flat and made from trees.
What are we? _____ boards _____

boards	planks	hoards

4. My _or_ sound is spelled _ore_.
I am between the land
and the sea. What am I? _____ shore _____

beach	store	shore

5. My _or_ sound is spelled _oor_.
You walk on me. What am I? _____ floor _____

poor	floor	grass

6. My _or_ sound is spelled _or_.
You can eat me when I am
soft and white. What am I? _____ popcorn _____

popcorn	cord	banana

7. My _or_ sound is spelled _our_.
I am part of a plant. I grow
on a vine. What am I? _____ gourd _____

leaf	gourd	mourn

8. My _or_ sound is spelled _or_.
If you're not careful, I can
stick you. What am I? _____ thorn _____

corn	thorn	pin

9. My _or_ sound is spelled _oar_.
I am a male pig. What other
name do I have? _____ boar _____

roar	hog	boar

Harcourt

Name_____

A Home on the Oregon Trail

Complete the sequence chart about "A Home on the Oregon Trail." Write a sentence in each box. The first box has been completed for you.

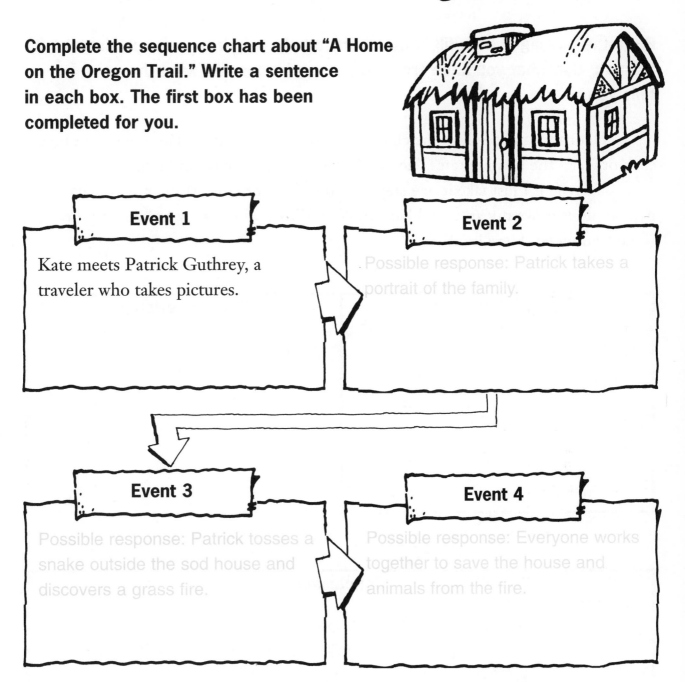

Event 1

Kate meets Patrick Guthrey, a traveler who takes pictures.

Event 2

Possible response: Patrick takes a portrait of the family.

Event 3

Possible response: Patrick tosses a snake outside the sod house and discovers a grass fire.

Event 4

Possible response: Everyone works together to save the house and animals from the fire.

Now use the information from the boxes to write a one-sentence summary of the selection.

Possible response: Kate and her family make a new friend who helps them

save their home from a grass fire.

Draw Conclusions

Read the passage. Then fill in the chart to help you draw a conclusion about Hannah. Use what you know from your experiences and what the passage tells you.

Hannah watched all of the children splashing each other. Two boys were racing each other to the floating raft. They looked as if they were having fun.

"Maybe if I just take it one step at a time I can do this. Mother says that all I need to do is move my arms and kick my legs. First I will just try holding my breath when I go under. Here I go!"

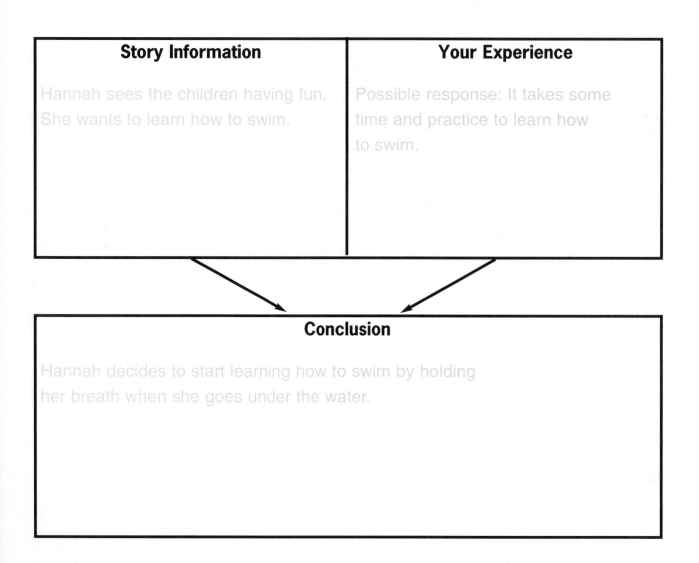

Story Information	Your Experience
Hannah sees the children having fun. She wants to learn how to swim.	Possible response: It takes some time and practice to learn how to swim.

Conclusion

Hannah decides to start learning how to swim by holding her breath when she goes under the water.

Harcourt

Fluency Builder

tutor	found	worried
glumly	around	her
impose	having	LaVerne
pastimes	hold	Pearl
irritably	some	pleasure
disposition	first	
bicker	sister	
grudge		

1. Pearl looked around glumly / and worried about sharing her room / with a new stepsister.

2. "Every summer!" / Pearl said irritably to herself.

3. Pearl found no pleasure / in having a new sister, / her happy disposition changed.

4. She felt that LaVerne / was imposing on her.

5. Pearl was holding a grudge / against her new stepsister.

6. At dinner, / the girls started / to bicker.

7. "I won't be surprised / if you find you like / some of the same pastimes," / said Pearl's stepfather.

8. At school / Pearl tutors the first graders / in reading.

Harcourt

Sisters Forever

Read the story below. Circle the words that have the same vowel sound as in *first*.

Sherman yearned for one perfect gift on his thirteenth birthday. He wanted a surfboard. His hands were a blur as he ripped into the first gift.

"It's a shirt. Thanks," he said. The next present was fake worms. Sherman thought this was a strange gift. He looked at Kurt, Herb, and Pearl. They were smirking. The last gift was a toy dirt bike.

"This is absurd!" Sherman said.

Herb giggled. "Okay, take the burlap cloth off that present in the corner." Under the burlap, Sherman spotted a new purple surfboard!

Sherman turned to his friends. "What a perfect gift! It was worth the wait. Thanks!"

Now read each question. Mark the letter for the best answer.

1. What day was it?
   A Thursday
   B Sherman's birthday
   C the first day of October
   D the third day of September

2. What did Sherman yearn for?
   A thirteen dollars
   B to learn to ski
   C a surfboard
   D fake worms

3. What was his first present?
   A a shirt
   B a small dirt bike
   C a turtle
   D fake worms

4. What present did Sherman find under the burlap?
   A a surfboard
   B a small dirt bike
   C a bird on a perch
   D a shirt

Sisters Forever

Write one sentence in each box below to show how Pearl and LaVerne went from disliking each other to getting along.

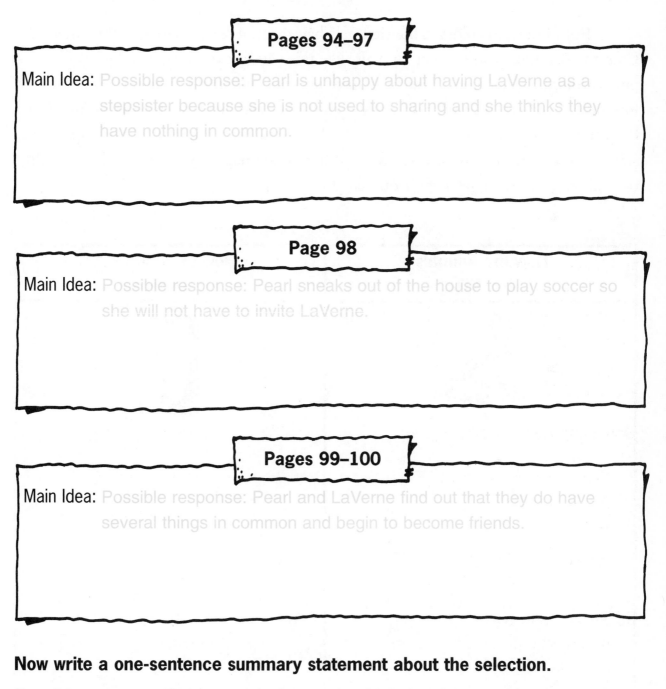

Pages 94–97

Main Idea: Possible response: Pearl is unhappy about having LaVerne as a stepsister because she is not used to sharing and she thinks they have nothing in common.

Page 98

Main Idea: Possible response: Pearl sneaks out of the house to play soccer so she will not have to invite LaVerne.

Pages 99–100

Main Idea: Possible response: Pearl and LaVerne find out that they do have several things in common and begin to become friends.

Now write a one-sentence summary statement about the selection.

Possible response: Two new stepsisters who think they have nothing in common find out that they do share several interests, and then they begin to be friends.

Compare and Contrast

Read the passage. Compare and contrast the two types of animals you read about.

Both hot- and cold-weather animals have special features that protect them from the outside. Hot-weather animals, like mice and jackrabbits, can dig underground to keep cool. They also have big ears and tails that help their bodies lose heat. Cold-weather animals, such as the polar bear, have thick coats of fur to keep them warm. These animals generally have small ears and tails. This helps them stay warm by trapping their body heat. Whether animals live where it is hot or cold, they all know how to get away from danger.

How the Animals Are Alike	How the Animals Are Different
Both have special features that protect them from the cold.	Hot-weather animals dig underground to stay cool.
Both know how to get away from danger.	Hot-weather animals have big ears and tails.
	Cold-weather animals have thick coats of fur to keep warm.
	Cold-weather animals have small ears and tails.

Harcourt

Fluency Builder

acquaintance	called	Mavis
scrounging	hungry	acorns
eavesdropping	any	Iris
excitable	believe	find
wistfully	they	dry
sympathetically		sadly
logical		menu
		idea

1. Mavis, / the jay, / and her acquaintance, / Iris, / the deer, / were picking through / a pile of dry leaves.

2. "I believe / it will be a long winter," / Mavis said / sadly.

3. Bo, / the wood rat, / was eavesdropping. / He said. / "My winter menu / will be acorns, / if I can find any!"

4. "When snow covers the leaves, / it makes it hard for you to eat, / Iris," / Mavis said / sympathetically.

5. "Yes, / I find myself / scrounging for food / and thinking wistfully / about spring," / said Iris.

6. "I have a logical plan!" / called Bo.

7. "If we all / work together, / we won't go hungry."

8. The idea / made the animals excitable. / They couldn't wait / for the acorns / to fall!

Oak Grove Picnic

Read the sentences and follow the directions.

1. It is a sunny day. Add the sun to the sky.

2. Tony is in the kitchen. Put an apron on him.

3. He has water in a mug. Put zebra stripes on the mug.

4. Tony will fry some potato pancakes. Circle the potatoes.

5. He also will make a salad. Add some slices of tomato to the bowl near Tony.

6. Tony's sister will help him. Give Amy a chef's hat.

7. Amy's apron is old. Rewrite her name on the apron.

8. Amy grinds some pepper. Add pepper to the bowl below the grinder.

For each word below, write a word from above that has the same long vowel sound and a similar spelling.

acorn _____apron_____   cold _____old_____

mind ___grinds, grinder___   sly _____fry, sky_____

Harcourt

Name _____

Oak Grove Picnic

Complete the sequence chart about "Oak Grove Picnic." Write a sentence or two in each box. The first box has been done for you.

Event 1 (Page 102)

Ruben, the squirrel, tells the other animals that the acorns are ripe and it's time to go to the oak grove.

Event 2 (Page 104)

Davis and Mavis rush off to get some acorns before they're all gone.

Event 3 (Page 105)

The owls follow the smaller animals to the oak grove, hoping to have a big lunch. Amy, the deer, says she is hungry for green leaves.

Event 4 (Pages 106–107)

Amy's mother explains why the oak trees are important to all the animals when winter comes. Then all the animals feast on acorns, and the owls go back home to sleep.

Use the information from the boxes above to write a one-sentence summary of the story.

Possible response: Ruben, the squirrel, spreads the news that the acorns are ready,

and the hungry animals of the oak woodlands enjoy an acorn feast before winter

comes.

Harcourt

Draw Conclusions

Read the passage. Then fill in the chart to help you draw a conclusion about Matt's actions.

"Easy out," shouted the kids in the outfield.

Matt watched Sam, his younger brother, step up to the plate. Matt was the best ball player around. Sam was the worst batter around. And today Matt's team was playing against Sam's. Sam looked so small standing there. Matt could hear his own teammates making fun of his brother.

Amazingly, Sam hit a pop fly. The ball headed straight for Matt. But Matt didn't raise his glove fast enough to catch the ball. As Sam reached first base, Matt gave his brother a thumbs-up. Then he just shrugged his shoulders at his angry teammates in the outfield.

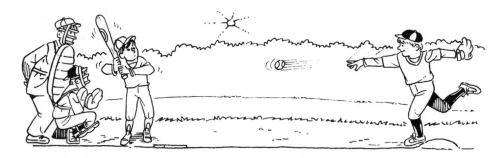

Story Information
Matt hears his teammates making fun of his brother Sam because he isn't a good ball player. They think he will be an easy out.
Your Own Knowledge
Possible response: it is not kind to make fun of other's abilities. Sometimes people surprise you.
Conclusion You Can Draw
Possible response: Matt was happy that his brother unexpectedly hit a pop fly and made it to first base.

Fluency Builder

hysterically
overwhelm
interpreter
appetizing
equivalent
irrigation
occasionally

letter
with
fun
think
food
many
bike
new

might
frightening
sights
flight
tries

1. Michelle's neighbor / is the interpreter / of Kim's letters.

2. Irrigation makes rice fields / muddy to walk in.

3. Michelle occasionally / tries to eat rice, / but having to eat it / with every meal / might overwhelm her.

4. Is a canoe / the equivalent / of a rowboat?

5. Kim had fun / seeing all / of the new sights / in Ho Chi Minh City.

6. Michelle thinks / many of the foods / in the market / sound appetizing.

7. It would be frightening / to ride a bike / next to so many cars.

8. Michelle was hysterically happy / when her mom agreed / to take a flight to Vietnam.

A Pen Pal in Vietnam

Read the story. Circle the words in which *igh* stands for the long *i* sound. Then draw a line under the words in which *ie* stands for the long *i* sound.

Last night Harry went to the fair. Two clowns wore bright helmets. Each tied a cloth to his helmet, one red and one blue. At first they pretended to fight. The red clown spilled ink on the blue clown's tights. The blue clown soaked the red clown with water from a hose. So the red clown dried himself with the blue clown's cape. Then

they both got on mighty horses. Each clown carried a whipped-cream pie. When they passed each other, they tossed the pies. Then Harry cried with delight when the whipped cream splattered on the clowns. Never before had he seen such a funny sight.

After the show was over, Harry had a bright idea. A clown's job might be just right for him! He tried on some tights and applied for a job at the fair.

Now write the long *i* word from above that best completes each sentence.

1. Each clown _____ a cloth to his helmet.

2. The blue clown's _____ had ink spilled on them.

3. The red clown _____ himself off with the blue clown's cape.

4. Both clowns rode on _____ horses.

5. Each carried a whipped-cream _____.

6. Harry had never before seen such a funny _____.

7. He thinks that being a clown _____ be fun.

A Pen Pal in Vietnam

Write one or two sentences in each box below
to tell how Michelle's life and Kim's life are
alike and different.

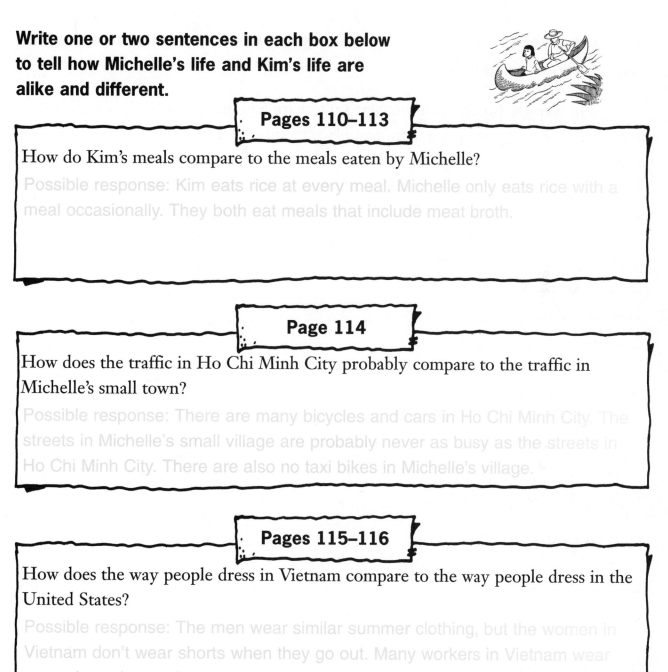

Pages 110–113

How do Kim's meals compare to the meals eaten by Michelle?

Possible response: Kim eats rice at every meal. Michelle only eats rice with a
meal occasionally. They both eat meals that include meat broth.

Page 114

How does the traffic in Ho Chi Minh City probably compare to the traffic in
Michelle's small town?

Possible response: There are many bicycles and cars in Ho Chi Minh City. The
streets in Michelle's small village are probably never as busy as the streets in
Ho Chi Minh City. There are also no taxi bikes in Michelle's village.

Pages 115–116

How does the way people dress in Vietnam compare to the way people dress in the
United States?

Possible response: The men wear similar summer clothing, but the women in
Vietnam don't wear shorts when they go out. Many workers in Vietnam wear
cone-shaped straw hats to protect their skin from the sun.

Use the information above to write a one-sentence summary about the selection.

Possible response: Despite many differences, Michelle and Kim lead

similar lives.

Name _____

Compare and Contrast

Read the passage. Then use the Venn diagram to compare and contrast the inventors you read about.

The Wright brothers and Robert Fulton are famous inventors. They all built machines that help people get from one place to another. On August 17, 1807, people in New York City were laughing at Fulton when his steamboat did not run at first. But the *Clermont* finally worked and made river travel important for America. Orville and Wilbur Wright looked to the sky to help people travel. On December 17, 1903, the first powered aircraft, *The Wright Flyer*, made four successful flights in Kitty Hawk, North Carolina. Although they had many failures, these inventors were also brave to keep trying. Possible responses are given.

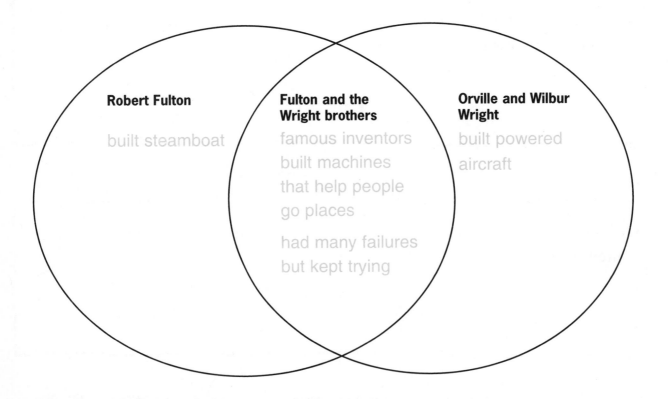

Robert Fulton

built steamboat

Fulton and the Wright brothers

famous inventors
built machines
that help people
go places

had many failures
but kept trying

Orville and Wilbur Wright

built powered
aircraft

Harcourt

Fluency Builder

tundra	sometimes	howls
piteously	across	power
surrender	when	amount
cease	between	down
abundant	tails	sounds
bonding	that	mouth
	may	snout

1. A wolf howls / across the tundra.

2. If a pack member dies, / all the other wolves / howl piteously.

3. Wolves squeak / when they are bonding / with each other.

4. Sometimes wolves use their tails / to communicate.

5. A wolf may hold / another wolf's snout / in its mouth.

6. There is an abundant amount / of communication / between wolves / in a pack.

7. When another wolf / meets an alpha wolf, / it holds its tail down, / to say that it is willing / to surrender its power / to the leader.

8. The sounds / of the wolves / will not cease to be heard / across the tundra.

Name _____

Wolf Pack: Sounds and Signals

Circle and write the word that makes the sentence tell about the picture.

1. Farmer May dug with her _____.

   (plow) scowl house

2. She came upon a big hole in the _____.

   spout grand (ground)

3. Farmer May wiped her _____.

   prow (brow) sound

4. "Did the _____ dig this hole?"

   (sow) clown sod

5. "Was it the _____?"

   prowl pouch (cow)

6. At that moment, a _____ ran by.

   frown (mouse) sprout

7. Farmer May heard a loud _____.

   chow (growl) scout

8. "It was my _____ that made

   town (hound) hand

   the hole in the ground!" she said.

Wolf Pack: Sounds and Signals

Write one or two sentences in each box below to show how wolves "talk" to each other.

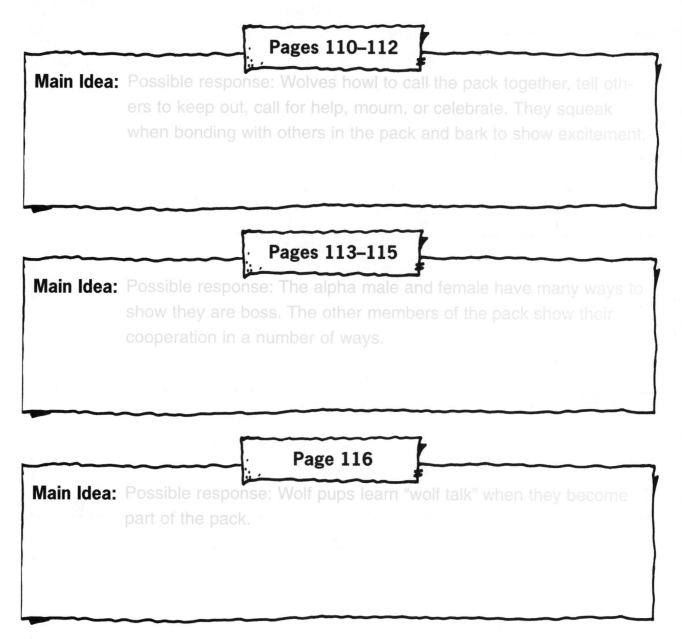

Pages 110–112

Main Idea: Possible response: Wolves howl to call the pack together, tell others to keep out, call for help, mourn, or celebrate. They squeak when bonding with others in the pack and bark to show excitement.

Pages 113–115

Main Idea: Possible response: The alpha male and female have many ways to show they are boss. The other members of the pack show their cooperation in a number of ways.

Page 116

Main Idea: Possible response: Wolf pups learn "wolf talk" when they become part of the pack.

Write a one-sentence summary statement about the selection.

Possible response: Wolves use many different sounds and signals to talk to each other as they work together to keep the pack strong.

Summarize

Read the passage. Then fill in the boxes below. Use what you wrote in the *Main Idea* and *Important Details* boxes to write a summary.

What is black and white and travels in a herd? Why, a zebra of course! Zebras are social animals just like wolves. They travel in groups in order to stay safe. Together, they have many eyes and ears to listen for their enemies. Zebras can also talk to each other and use facial expressions to show how they feel. If a zebra gets separated from the group, the others will search for it until it is found. A herd of zebras is like a big family of animals.

Main Idea

Possible response: Zebras are social animals.

Important Details

Possible responses: travel in groups; can talk to each other and express feelings; will search for missing members of the herd.

Summary

Possible response. Zebras are social animals that live in herds. They communicate and cooperate with each other. A herd is like a big family.

Fluency Builder

document   because   pencils
prosthetic   hold   device
device   their   ice
disabilities   them   space
circular   want   places
scholarship   already
modify   new
    idea

1. Ernest Hamwi invented a cone / with a circular opening / to hold ice cream.

2. Two men invented pencils / with erasers / on the end of them.

3. The shopping cart / was invented / because shoppers needed / more space in their baskets.

4. Puzzles were invented / to help children / learn about places / around the world.

5. You may want to modify / an invention / that is already in use.

6. A new prosthetic device / can help people / with disabilities.

7. A patent / is a document / that protects your idea.

8. Taking the time / to find out / how to make / your invention better / is a sign / of good scholarship.

Name _____

Who Invented This?

Read the story. Circle all the words in which *c* stands for the /s/ sound.

Cecil lives in Cedar Falls. Bruce is his cat.

His family has a home outside the city. He thinks it is a fine place.

His home has a cellar. Bruce looks for mice.

Cecil likes to race his bicycle everywhere.

He goes to the Cinema Palace, where a ticket costs just fifty cents.

Cecil likes to see films about outer space.

Circle and write the word that best completes each sentence.

1. Cecil's cat is named ____Bruce____. **Brenda** **Bruce** **Brute**

2. Cecil lives near the ____city____. **circus** **city** **pace**

3. His home has a ____cellar____. **corridor** **spice** **cellar**

4. He rides his ____bicycle____ everywhere. **cyclops** **bicycle** **cyclist**

5. At the Cinema Palace, tickets cost just fifty ____cents____.

        cents **peace** **cans**

6. He likes movies about outer ____space____ best.

        space **fence** **specks**

Name _____

Who Invented This?

In each box below, name the invention and describe what it does.

Page 126

Invention: pencil with its own eraser

What It Does: Possible response: It keeps the eraser and the pencil together.

Page 127

Invention: shopping cart

What It Does: Possible response: It lets you get more food at the supermarket.

Page 128

Invention: ice-cream cone

What It Does: Possible response: It holds ice cream and you can eat it.

Page 129

Invention: picture puzzle

What It Does: Possible response: It teaches children where places are around the world.

Page 130

Invention: safety pin

What It Does: Possible response: It holds things together without sticking the user.

Write a one-sentence summary about the selection.

Possible response: Inventors can solve problems by inventing things.

Main Idea and Details

Read the following paragraph as you think about which sentence states the main idea, or what the paragraph is mainly about. Then fill in the chart. Each detail should be one idea from the paragraph. Possible responses are shown.

Our School Playground

Our school playground is a great place to play. It has a climbing tower to hang from. It has long, short, and tunnel slides. It even has a rope bridge! My favorite place on the playground is the fire pole because I can slide down it faster than anyone I know!

Main Idea
Our school playground is a great place to play.

Detail	Detail
It has a climbing tower.	It has short, long, and tunnel slides.
Detail	**Detail**
It has a rope bridge.	It has a fire pole.

Fluency Builder

muttered	see	fudge
strengthening	come	village
sculptor	work	gentle
straightaway	find	giant
retorted	talk	large
alibi	found	Gina
	they	Angela

1. Gina Ginetti is a well-known / girl detective.

2. All of the citizens had come / to the village square / to see the work / of a local sculptor revealed.

3. The Gentle Giant is / Fudge Corners's best-known dog.

4. "I don't see / what all the fuss is about," / Al muttered.

5. "Let's find Reggie / and talk to him / straightaway," / said Gina.

6. Al found / the support of Gina / and Angela strengthening / and they searched the large crowd.

7. "I have an alibi / for last night," / Reggie retorted.

8. How did Gina know / that Reggie had stolen / Al's statue?

The Case of the Strange Sculptor

Write the word that answers each riddle.

1. I begin like *giraffe*. I make things taste good. What am I?

ginger

garnish   ginger   giant

2. I begin like *gentle*. You can play basketball inside me. What am I?

gym

gym   garage   gem

3. I begin like *general*. I am very, very smart. What am I?

genius

grown-up   gem   genius

4. I have the same *g* sound as in *original*. I help cars go. What am I?

engine

page   gas   engine

5. I end like *judge*. I can help you cross a river. What am I?

bridge

nudge   bridge   wagon

6. I have the sound that the letter *g* stands for in *clergy*. I can make you sick. What am I?

germ

germ   sugar   gentle

7. I end like *badge*. I am like a big bush. What am I?

hedge

fidget   hedge   garden

8. I have the sound that the letter *g* stands for in *change*. I am someone you don't know. Who am I?

stranger

stranger   gardener   hinge

9. I have the sound that the letter *g* stands for in *large*. I tell how old you are. What am I?

age

energy   gift   age

Harcourt

Name_____

The Case of the Strange Sculptor

Write one or two sentences in each box below to sum up the story. Be sure to write the events in correct order.

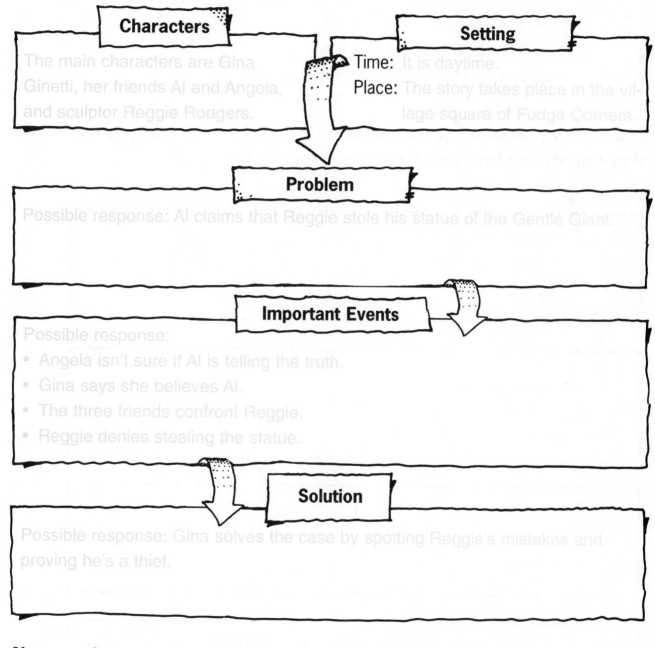

Characters

The main characters are Gina Ginetti, her friends Al and Angela, and sculptor Reggie Rodgers.

Setting

Time: It is daytime.
Place: The story takes place in the village square of Fudge Corners.

Problem

Possible response: Al claims that Reggie stole his statue of the Gentle Giant.

Important Events

Possible response:
• Angela isn't sure if Al is telling the truth.
• Gina says she believes Al.
• The three friends confront Reggie.
• Reggie denies stealing the statue.

Solution

Possible response: Gina solves the case by spotting Reggie's mistakes and proving he's a thief.

Now use the story map to write a one-sentence summary of the story.

When Reggie Rodgers steals Al's statue of the Gentle Giant and presents it

as his own, Gina must use her detective skills to prove that Reggie is a thief.

Name _____

Sequence

These sentences are not in the correct sequence.

Then, he removes the bubble wand and holds it in front of his mouth.
First, Luis opens the bottle of bubbles.
Finally, the air around Luis is filled with bubbles.
Next, Luis takes a deep breath and blows.

Write the sentences in the correct order to complete the diagram. Circle the signal words that help you understand the sequence.

First, Luis opens the bottle of bubbles.

Then, he removes the bubble wand and holds it in front of his mouth.

Next, Luis takes a deep breath and blows.

Finally, the air around Luis is filled with bubbles.

Harcourt

Fluency Builder

thrifty	upon	coin
generous	all	annoyed
roguish	from	oinking
rascally	when	toiled
fascinated	there	soiled
	hens	joyfully
	pigs	
	away	
	his	

1. The farmer was thrifty / and he insisted / upon saving every coin.

2. The farmer saved / a generous fortune.

3. He became fascinated / by all of his riches.

4. The farmer's rascally friend / made up a roguish plan / to stop the farmer / from boasting.

5. When the farmer toiled / in his fields / his clothes became soiled / and his face was wet.

6. When the farmer purchased / more pigs and hens, / there was a lot / of extra oinking and clucking / on his farm.

7. The farmer became annoyed / with his friend.

8. The farmer joyfully gave away / the fields, / the pigs, / and the hens / that were making him unhappy.

Just Enough Is Plenty

Mark the answer in front of the sentence that tells about the picture.

1 **A** Roy has a coil of rope.
  B Roy digs in the soil.
  C Roy has a royal hat.
  D Roy makes his choice.

2 **A** Dan eats some oysters.
  B Dan has a gold coin.
  C Dan's lunch is spoiled now.
  D Dan looks for the foil.

3 **A** Gwen is annoyed by the bee.
  B The bee destroys Gwen's snack.
  C Gwen enjoys her blocks.
  D Gwen joins a club with Roy.

4 **A** He boils broth in a pot.
  B That cloth is soiled.
  C He hears a noise in the corner.
  D He is disappointed by the rain.

5 **A** Liz points at Roy.
  B Liz uncoils the rope.
  C Liz embroiders her name.
  D Liz has a soiled hat.

6 **A** Brinda gives a coin to the boy.
  B Brinda loiters by the exit.
  C Brinda's bike is destroyed.
  D Brinda avoids the soiled rug.

Name _____

Just Enough Is Plenty

Complete the story map to help you summarize the story. Be sure to write the events in the correct order.

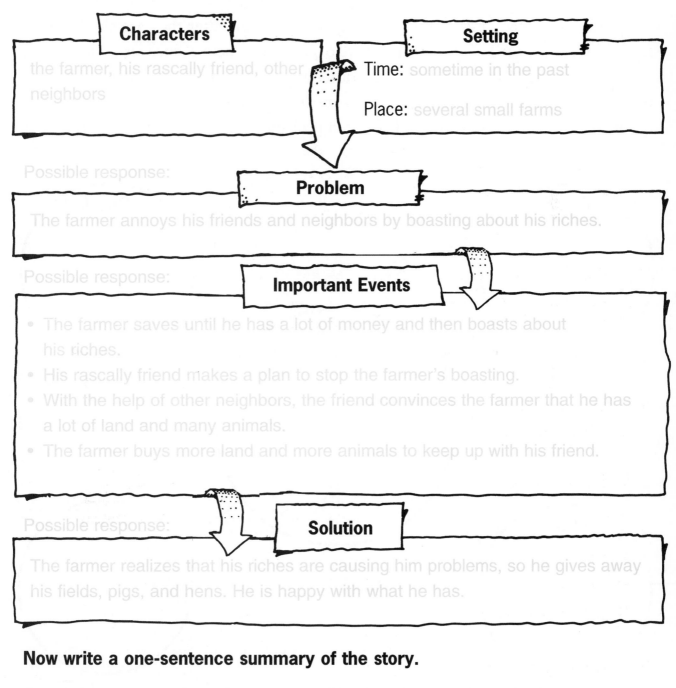

Characters

the farmer, his rascally friend, other neighbors

Setting

Time: sometime in the past

Place: several small farms

Possible response:

Problem

The farmer annoys his friends and neighbors by boasting about his riches.

Possible response:

Important Events

- The farmer saves until he has a lot of money and then boasts about his riches.
- His rascally friend makes a plan to stop the farmer's boasting.
- With the help of other neighbors, the friend convinces the farmer that he has a lot of land and many animals.
- The farmer buys more land and more animals to keep up with his friend.

Possible response:

Solution

The farmer realizes that his riches are causing him problems, so he gives away his fields, pigs, and hens. He is happy with what he has.

Now write a one-sentence summary of the story.

Possible response: A thrifty farmer's tricky friend teaches him that being happy

with what you have is more satisfying than working very hard to be rich.

Name

Main Idea and Details

Read the paragraph and identify the main idea and details. Complete the web. Possible responses are given.

Trees have many uses, both when they are living and after they are cut down. Because trees use carbon dioxide and make oxygen, they help reduce air pollution. Trees also provide habitats for birds and other animals. Both people and animals get food from many kinds of trees. After trees are cut down, we use them for many products including paper and wood. You can probably think of many other uses, too.

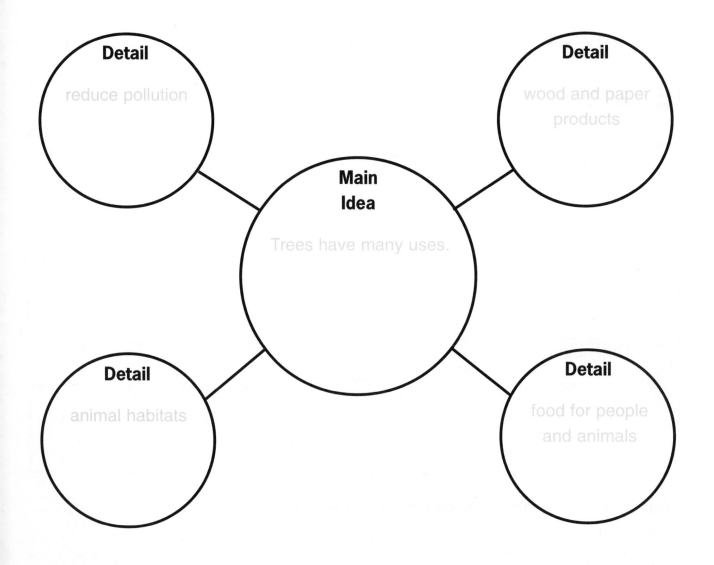

Detail

reduce pollution

Detail

wood and paper products

Main Idea

Trees have many uses.

Detail

animal habitats

Detail

food for people and animals

Fluency Builder

script   yell   because
triumphantly   you're   caught
desperately   that's   yawn
injustice   I've   dawn
repentant   lost   awful
acceptable   lawyer
discards   fault
circumstances

1. Eating is usually acceptable, / unless you're the Big Bad Wolf / trying to eat a grandmother.

2. Judge Bo Peep exclaimed, / "That's awful!"

3. "I've been up since dawn," / she said with a yawn, / "and I've got lost sheep / that have to be caught."

4. The lawyer triumphantly yelled, / "You see? / He did it!"

5. The Big Bad Wolf / was not even repentant / of his crime.

6. The Big Bad Wolf cried, / "This is an injustice. / It's the author's fault / because he wrote the script."

7. The wolf desperately claimed / he was a victim of circumstances.

8. The wolf discards / the testimony / of Red Riding Cap.

Harcourt

Name _____

Big Bad Wolf and the Law

Read the sentences and do what they tell you.

1. Dawn and Paula are having a picnic. Draw a picnic basket on the blanket.
2. Give Dawn a straw so she can drink her milk.
3. The hawk caught a garden snake. Put a small snake in the hawk's claws.
4. Draw some leaves on the lawn under the tree.
5. Don't let the dripping water go to waste! Put a bucket under the faucet.
6. The dog is bored. Draw a toy between its paws so it can play.
7. Some ants are crawling to the picnic basket. Draw a line of ants on the blanket.
8. The fawn is eating berries from the hedge. Give the fawn more berries to eat.

Now circle the words that have the vowel sound you hear in _saw_ and _taught_.

Harcourt

Big Bad Wolf and the Law

Complete the story map below to summarize the selection. Be sure to write the events in correct order.

Characters

bailiff, Judge Bo Peep, Red Riding Cap, the lawyer, and Big Bad Wolf

Setting

Time: August

Place: Storyland Court

Problem

Possible response:

Big Bad Wolf is on trial after being accused of "attempted eating."

Important Events

Possible responses:

- The lawyer explains the charges against Wolf, but Wolf denies trying to eat the grandmother and granddaughter.
- Red Riding Cap claims that the wolf said her grandma would be delicious.
- The judge is distracted by worry about her sheep.
- Wolf claims his bad behavior is the author's fault, since the author wrote the script.

Solution

Possible response:

Wolf almost convinces the judge that he's harmless. At the last minute, though, the lawyer asks to call the three little pigs to the stand, and Wolf knows he'll be convicted.

Use the story map above to write a one-sentence summary of the story.

Possible response: Wolf tries to persuade the other characters that he seems bad

only because the author made him that way, but he's sure to fail when the three

little pigs take the stand.

Harcourt

Sequence

Read the following paragraph and identify the sequence of events.

There once was a girl who was locked up in a tower so high that it reached the clouds. The girl knew no way to escape her fate. There was nothing for her to do all day but watch her hair grow longer and longer and longer. One morning, as she was brushing her hair, she crafted a clever plan to escape. First, she tied her hair into a long braid. Next, she managed to cut the braid off with a sharp rock in the tower. Then, she tied the braid to a table in the room. Finally, she threw the rest of the braid out the window toward the ground. After she climbed down her clever rope, she ran bald-headed all throughout the town!

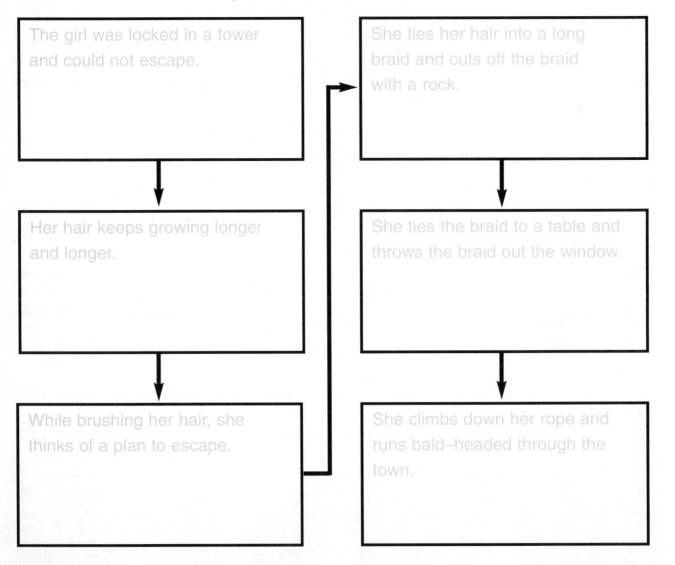

The girl was locked in a tower and could not escape.

She ties her hair into a long braid and cuts off the braid with a rock.

Her hair keeps growing longer and longer.

She ties the braid to a table and throws the braid out the window.

While brushing her hair, she thinks of a plan to escape.

She climbs down her rope and runs bald–headed through the town.

Harcourt

Name _____

Fluency Builder

decreed	through	good
famine	king	Woodlandia
implored	many	firewood
trickled	old	looked
plentifully	was	books
	work	should
	down	would
		shook

1. The good kingdom / of Woodlandia / was free from famine / for many years.

2. The kingdom was also / plentifully supplied / with firewood.

3. King Roger decreed / that all of his subjects / should dress exactly like him.

4. How could they dress / like the king?

5. The Woodlandians / implored the ministers, / "Please tell us / what we should do!"

6. The ministers / looked through / rare old books / of wisdom, / hoping to find a solution.

7. Would their clever plan / work?

8. King Roger shook / with laughter / until tears trickled / down his cheeks.

Harcourt

A Clever Plan

Read the story. Circle the words that have the vowel sound you hear in *took* and *would*.

Woody and Eric are packing for a hike. They will cross the woods on foot. They hope to camp by a brook. Woody grabs a camping book. "Should I take this book?" he asks.

Eric looks at it. "Yes. It would tell us what to do if we got lost."

"Good thinking," Woody tells him. "What else should I take?"

"Snacks," Eric says, "and a wool jacket to keep warm."

"You are good at this," Woody tells him.

Eric says, "It gets easy with practice."

Woody's backpack is stuffed, but he wants to take two more things. "Eric, could you take the football and the extra raisins?" he asks.

Eric looks in his pack and frowns. "I have space for only one of them. What should I do?"

Woody smiles. "Leave the football," he says. "We may need the extra raisins for energy."

Eric tells him, "You know, you are good at this, too."

Now write the circled word that best completes each sentence.

1. Eric and Woody will travel on _____ foot _____ across the woods.

2. They hope to camp by a _____ brook _____.

3. Eric tells Woody to take the camping _____ book _____.

4. He also tells Woody to pack snacks and a _____ wool _____ jacket.

5. Woody thinks Eric is _____ good _____ at deciding what to pack.

6. Eric frowns after he _____ looks _____ in his pack.

7. The raisins or the _____ football _____ can fit, but not both.

8. Woody thinks they _____ should _____ leave the football.

Harcourt

A Clever Plan

Write sentences in each box below to summarize the story. Be sure to write the events in the correct order.

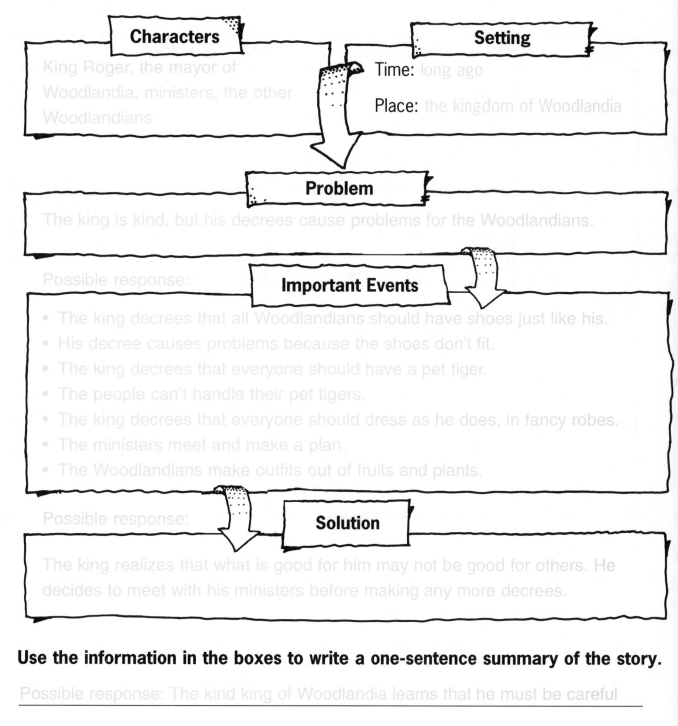

Characters

King Roger, the mayor of Woodlandia, ministers, the other Woodlandians

Setting

Time: long ago

Place: the kingdom of Woodlandia

Problem

The king is kind, but his decrees cause problems for the Woodlandians.

Important Events

Possible response:

- The king decrees that all Woodlandians should have shoes just like his.
- His decree causes problems because the shoes don't fit.
- The king decrees that everyone should have a pet tiger.
- The people can't handle their pet tigers.
- The king decrees that everyone should dress as he does, in fancy robes.
- The ministers meet and make a plan.
- The Woodlandians make outfits out of fruits and plants.

Solution

Possible response:

The king realizes that what is good for him may not be good for others. He decides to meet with his ministers before making any more decrees.

Use the information in the boxes to write a one-sentence summary of the story.

Possible response: The kind king of Woodlandia learns that he must be careful

with his royal decrees so that he doesn't cause problems for his people.

Harcourt

Compare and Contrast

Think about how "One Grain of Rice" and "A Clever Plan" are alike and different. Fill in the chart. Use the chart to help you answer the questions.

Story	"One Grain of Rice"	"A Clever Plan"
Characters	Rani the raja	King Roger mayor of Woodlandia ministers Woodlandians
Setting	long ago India	long ago the kingdom of Woodlandia
Plot	The raja's decree causes the people of India to go hungry. Rani's cleverness saves her people.	The king's decrees cause problems for the Woodlandians.
Lesson	Possible response: Leaders should be wise and fair.	Possible response: What's good for one is not necessarily good for everyone else.

1. How are the settings of the stories alike? _Both stories take place long ago._

2. How are the settings different? _One story takes place in a real country._ _The other takes place in an imaginary country._

3. How are the plots of the stories alike? _A leader's decree causes problems for_ _his people._

Fluency Builder

dedication   old   true

billowing   animal   renews

brigade   again   new

ventilate   very   fireproof

flammable   near   soon

curfew   after   too

    come

    sometimes

1. Old trees / are very flammable, / and even new shoots / are not fireproof.

2. High winds / can ventilate a fire / and send up / billowing flames.

3. When a fire / is near a camp, / rangers set a curfew.

4. New members / of a fire brigade / soon show / their dedication.

5. But / sometimes / it takes a big rainstorm / to put out a fire.

6. It is true / that fire / renews a forest.

7. After a fire, / the animals / come back.

8. Plants / grow again, / too.

Name _____

Fire in the Forest

**Make the sentences tell about the pictures. Circle and write
the words that have the same vowel sound as in *blue*.**

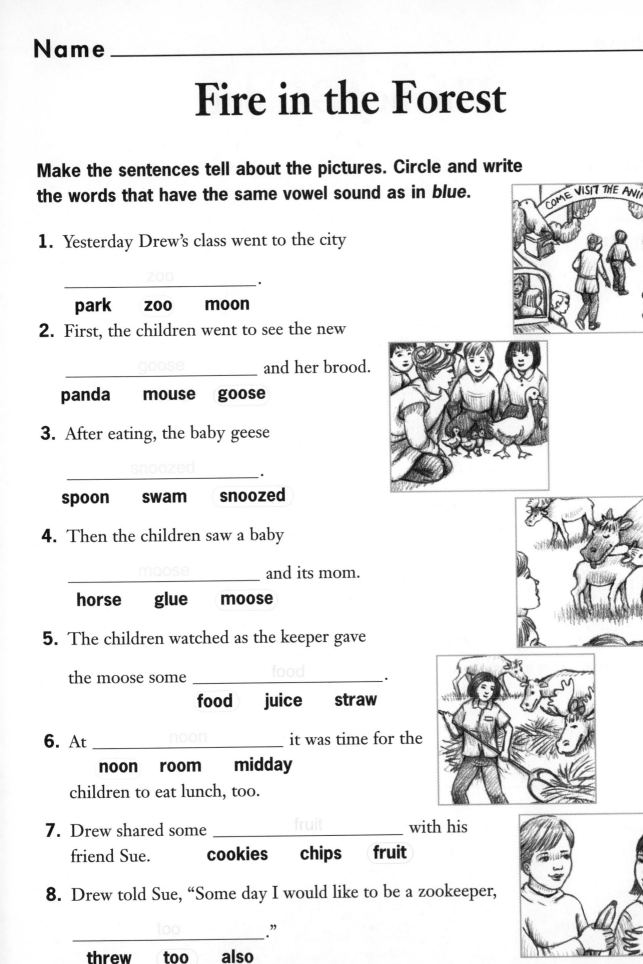

1. Yesterday Drew's class went to the city

   _____ .

   park   zoo   moon

2. First, the children went to see the new

   _____ and her brood.

   panda   mouse   (goose)

3. After eating, the baby geese

   _____ .

   spoon   swam   (snoozed)

4. Then the children saw a baby

   _____ and its mom.

   horse   glue   (moose)

5. The children watched as the keeper gave

   the moose some _____ .

   (food)   juice   straw

6. At _____ it was time for the

   noon   room   midday

   children to eat lunch, too.

7. Drew shared some _____ with his

   friend Sue.   **cookies   chips   (fruit)**

8. Drew told Sue, "Some day I would like to be a zookeeper,

   _____ ."

   threw   (too)   also

Harcourt

Fire in the Forest

Write one sentence in each box below to tell what you learned in "Fire in the Forest."

Pages 166–167

Main Idea: Possible response: Forest rangers now think that fires are an important part of a forest's life cycle because they help the forest renew itself.

Pages 168–169

Main Idea: Possible response: Rangers and firefighters face a difficult challenge in deciding when to fight a forest fire.

Page 170

Main Idea: Possible response: Though the Yellowstone fires of the summer of 1988 burned millions of trees, they did not destroy the forest.

Use the information above to write a one-sentence summary statement about the selection.

Possible response: Forest fires are an important part of a forest's life cycle, as was shown by the Yellowstone fires during the summer of 1988.

Harcourt

Elements of Nonfiction: Text Structure

Read the following nonfiction passage and identify the text structure.

March 1, 1872, was an important day for nature lovers. That was the day President Grant signed the bill that made Yellowstone the world's first national park. In 1894 Congress passed a law that protected the park's wildlife. In 1972 the park held a big celebration for its 100th birthday. Today tourists enjoy many different activities in Yellowstone.

In what kind of text structure are events told in the order in which they happened? Circle your answer in the box below.

compare and contrast	main idea and details	sequence of events

Fill in the chart with what happened on each date.

March 1, 1872 Yellowstone became a national park.

↓

1894 Congress passed a law protecting the park's wildlife.

↓

1972 The park celebrated its 100th birthday.

↓

Today Tourists enjoy many activities in Yellowstone.

Fluency Builder

enrich	were	from
petitioners	to	world
obliged	who	come
examiner	their	gnawed
apologized	some	know
certificate	said	written
resounded	here	

1. The hall resounded / with the noise / of the people talking.

2. Petitioners / from all over the world / were waiting / to know their future.

3. First / they were obliged / to see / an examiner.

4. The examiners / checked a written certificate / for each person.

5. A bad feeling / gnawed at the petitioners / as they waited / for a doctor.

6. They had learned / that some doctors / were forced to apologize.

7. "We regret / that you cannot stay here," / the doctors said to immigrants / who were sick.

8. Those who were allowed to come in / enriched their lives / in the United States.

Name _____

A Place of New Beginnings

Circle and write the word that answers each riddle.

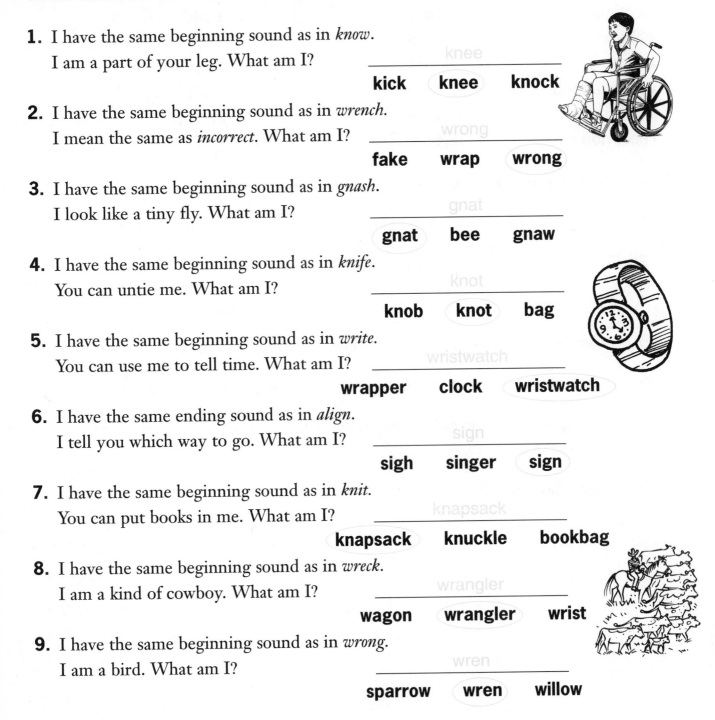

1. I have the same beginning sound as in *know*.
I am a part of your leg. What am I? _____ knee _____

                 kick   (knee)   knock

2. I have the same beginning sound as in *wrench*.
I mean the same as *incorrect*. What am I? _____ wrong _____

                 fake   wrap   (wrong)

3. I have the same beginning sound as in *gnash*.
I look like a tiny fly. What am I? _____ gnat _____

                 (gnat)   bee   gnaw

4. I have the same beginning sound as in *knife*.
You can untie me. What am I? _____ knot _____

                 knob   (knot)   bag

5. I have the same beginning sound as in *write*.
You can use me to tell time. What am I? _____ wristwatch _____

                 wrapper   clock   (wristwatch)

6. I have the same ending sound as in *align*.
I tell you which way to go. What am I? _____ sign _____

                 sigh   singer   (sign)

7. I have the same beginning sound as in *knit*.
You can put books in me. What am I? _____ knapsack _____

                 (knapsack)   knuckle   bookbag

8. I have the same beginning sound as in *wreck*.
I am a kind of cowboy. What am I? _____ wrangler _____

                 wagon   (wrangler)   wrist

9. I have the same beginning sound as in *wrong*.
I am a bird. What am I? _____ wren _____

                 sparrow   (wren)   willow

Harcourt

Name _____

A Place of New Beginnings

Complete the main-idea chart to tell what Karen discovers in "A Place of New Beginnings." Write a sentence in each box. The first one has been done for you.

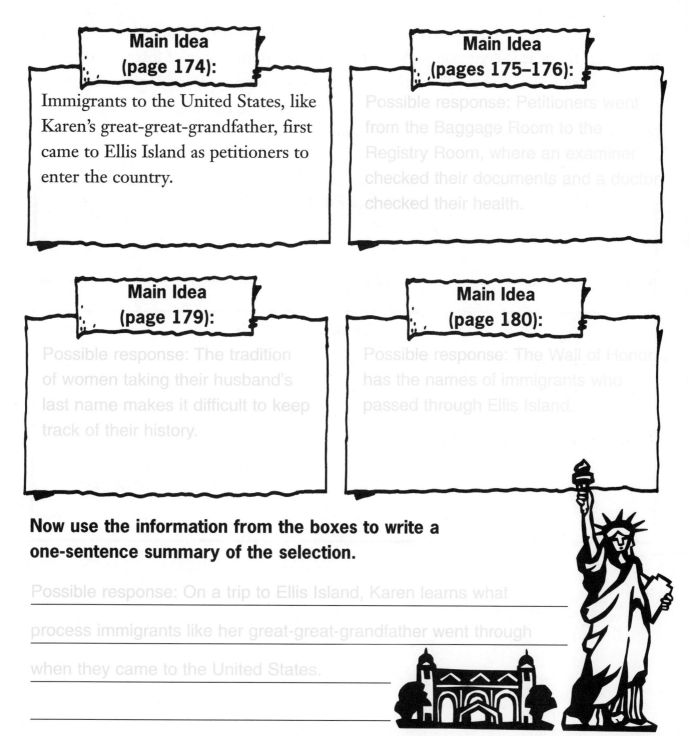

Main Idea (page 174):

Immigrants to the United States, like Karen's great-great-grandfather, first came to Ellis Island as petitioners to enter the country.

Main Idea (pages 175–176):

Possible response: Petitioners went from the Baggage Room to the Registry Room, where an examiner checked their documents and a doctor checked their health.

Main Idea (page 179):

Possible response: The tradition of women taking their husband's last name makes it difficult to keep track of their history.

Main Idea (page 180):

Possible response: The Wall of Honor has the names of immigrants who passed through Ellis Island.

Now use the information from the boxes to write a one-sentence summary of the selection.

Possible response: On a trip to Ellis Island, Karen learns what process immigrants like her great-great-grandfather went through when they came to the United States.

Author's Purpose

Read the passage. Decide if the author is writing to inform, to entertain, or to persuade. Then fill in the chart with the details that helped you determine the author's purpose. Possible responses are shown.

Our country is beautiful. But in many places the beauty is hidden. It is hidden by piles of litter. It is every citizen's job to keep our country free of litter. Good citizens do not litter! They throw things away in the proper places. If you want to keep our country beautiful, you should stop littering. You can even lead a monthly neighborhood cleanup. Please keep our country clean!

Author's Purpose
to persuade

Details
1. Good citizens do not litter!
2. If you want to keep our country beautiful, you should stop littering.
3. Please keep our country clean!

Harcourt

Fluency Builder

spiny	flower	phase
topple	find	photograph
decomposes	many	geography
brush	would	rough
habitat	you	tough
teeming	from	enough
perch		
nectar		

1. Do you think / taking photographs / in the desert / would be dull?

2. You might be surprised / to learn / that the desert's rough geography, / is teeming / with interesting life forms.

3. The desert / is a fine habitat / for plants and animals / that are tough enough / to survive there.

4. If you look closely / at a tall, spiny cactus, / you might see a tiny bird / sipping nectar / from a cactus flower.

5. Old cactuses topple / and decompose / into interesting shapes.

6. At noon / you may find animals / escaping from the heat / in the shade / of scrubby desert brush.

7. Some insects / spend a phase of their life / under the ground, / but many / can be seen in plain sight.

8. Bats perch in caves by day, / but you can photograph them / when they leave their caves / at dusk.

Desert Animals

Read the letter. Then read each question that follows. Circle the letter of the best answer choice.

Dear Ralph,

In class today we talked about different inventions that have helped people express themselves. Before the first alphabet was invented, people wrote using pictographs, or simple drawings. Among the first written words were drawings of stars and animals.

Alfred Vail helped Samuel Morse invent the code for the telegraph. Alexander Graham Bell invented the telephone in 1876.

The phonograph was invented by Thomas Edison in 1877. A phonograph was a machine that played recorded music.

I wonder who invented laughter. It's my favorite way to express myself. When things get tough, laughing often helps me feel better.

Write back soon!

Your friend,

Phyllis

1 What did Alexander Graham Bell invent?

A telegraph

B television

C roughness

D telephone

2 Morse and Vail invented a code for the ___.

A telephone

B elephant

C photograph

D telegraph

3 Before there was an ___, people wrote using pictographs.

A algebra

B alphabet

C autograph

D pharmacy

4 Phyllis wants to know who invented ___.

A rough

B elephants

C graphs

D laughter

Harcourt

Desert Animals

Write one sentence in each box below to show what you learned about desert animals.

Pages 182–183

What surprises does the desert hold? Possible response: It looks dry and barren, but it is actually a home to many creatures that have adapted to its climate.

Pages 184–186

What might you find if you look closely? Possible response: You might find insects, lizards, land-dwelling turtles, rattlesnakes, and jackrabbits.

Pages 187–188

What other creatures make their homes in the desert? Possible response: The desert is home to hummingbirds, roadrunners, buzzards, bats, and coyotes.

Use the information above to write a one-sentence summary of the selection.

Possible response: The desert may look empty, but it is actually filled with

many kinds of animals that live there.

Elements of Nonfiction: Text Structure

Read the paragraphs. Then answer the questions.

Rodeo Week

Every year, our town has Rodeo Week. On Monday, the cowhands arrive. On Tuesday, the rodeo events begin. The big event on Wednesday is bronco busting. Thursday is the day for children's races and games. Rodeo Week ends with a square dance on Friday.

Summer Vacation

During summer vacation, my life stays the same in some ways and changes in other ways. I still get to spend time with my friends, but I see them at day camp instead of at school. Instead of reading schoolbooks, I read mystery stories. During summer vacation, I still have to help around the house. I have more free time, though, because I don't have homework.

1. In what kind of text structure are events told in time order? _____

_____

2. What kind of text structure shows how things are alike and different?

3. What kind of text structure does "Rodeo Week" have? _____

_____

4. What kind of text structure does "Summer Vacation" have? _____

_____

Fluency Builder

undoubtedly	know	Heather
loathe	little	dread
certainty	through	sleepyhead
protruded	wasn't	sweater
indifferent	food	breakfast
sulkily	pulled	ready
heartily	said	

1. Heather woke / with a feeling / of dread.

2. "I just know / I'm going to loathe / school here," / she told herself / with certainty.

3. "Rise and shine, / sleepyhead!" / her mother / called out / heartily.

4. "Oh, Mom!" / Heather said / sulkily.

5. She pulled on / her sweater / as she got ready / for school.

6. Her cat / had finished washing himself, / but a little tip of pink / still protruded / from his mouth.

7. Undoubtedly / she would make it / through the day, / but she wasn't / looking forward to it.

8. Heather / normally enjoyed breakfast, / but today / she felt indifferent / to food.

Name _____

School Days

Read the story. Circle all the words that have the vowel sound that you hear in *head* spelled *ea*.

After breakfast Rick and Yoshi packed for a picnic.
"I'm making healthful sandwiches," said Rick.
Yoshi said, "Don't forget the gingerbread cake!"
The boys hiked up a hill to a grassy meadow. When they got to the top, they were out of breath and sweating.
"This looks like a good spot," Rick said. He spread out a blanket on the grass.
Yoshi looked at the sky. Dark clouds were coming closer.
"The weather is going to be dreadful," Yoshi said. "I don't think we'll have time to finish all of our lunch before it rains. Should we have the sandwiches or the gingerbread cake first?"
The boys smiled at one another. "The cake!" they said.

Circle and write the word that best completes each sentence.

1. The boys made sandwiches after _____breakfast_____.

   dinner   **headlights**   **breakfast**

2. Yoshi reminded Rick to pack the _____gingerbread_____ cake.

   headphones   **gingerbread**   **treasure**

3. A _____meadow_____ was at the top of the hill.
   thread   **meadow**   **shortbread**

4. The boys were _____breathless_____ after the hike.

   breathless   **helpless**   **ready**

5. Rick _____spread_____ out a blanket on the grass.

   spread   **unread**   **red**

6. Yoshi said the weather was going to be _____dreadful_____.

   perfect   **healthy**   **dreadful**

Harcourt

School Days

Complete each box below to summarize the selection. Be sure to write the events in the correct order.

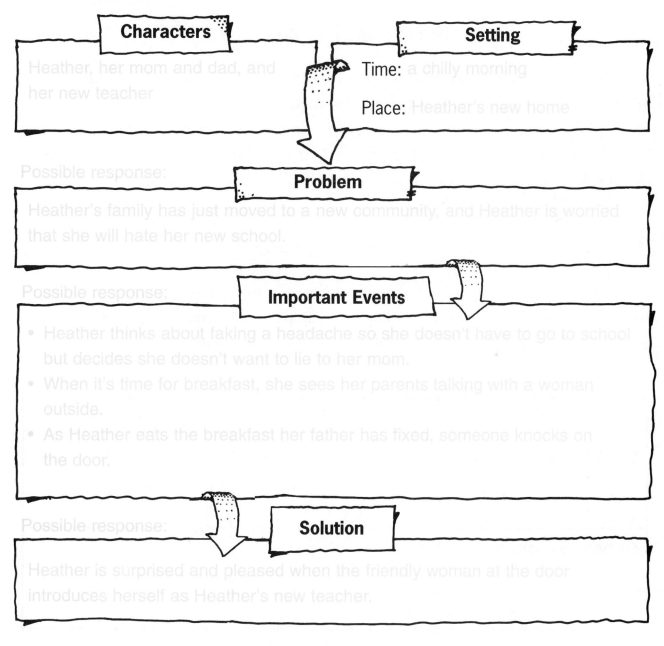

Characters

Heather, her mom and dad, and her new teacher

Setting

Time: a chilly morning

Place: Heather's new home

Possible response:

Problem

Heather's family has just moved to a new community, and Heather is worried that she will hate her new school.

Possible response:

Important Events

• Heather thinks about faking a headache so she doesn't have to go to school but decides she doesn't want to lie to her mom.

• When it's time for breakfast, she sees her parents talking with a woman outside.

• As Heather eats the breakfast her father has fixed, someone knocks on the door.

Possible response:

Solution

Heather is surprised and pleased when the friendly woman at the door introduces herself as Heather's new teacher.

Use the story map above to write a one-sentence summary of the story.

Possible response: Although she is unhappy at first about her first day at a

new school, Heather's mood improves when she meets her new teacher.

Harcourt

Author's Purpose

Read each paragraph. Think about the author's purpose for writing and his or her perspective. Then fill in the chart.

Don't Forget Your Breakfast

Eating a healthy breakfast is a good way to start your day. A healthful breakfast gives you energy. When you eat something like cereal with milk and fruit, you already have a good start on getting the vitamins and minerals you need for the day. If you don't eat a healthful breakfast, you may feel tired and grumpy. The few minutes you spend eating breakfast will pay off all day long. Start your day with a good breakfast.

German Shepherds

The German shepherd is a very smart dog. German shepherds can be trained to be police dogs. They can also be trained to help people. German shepherds are often used as guide dogs for the blind and as search-and-rescue dogs.

Title	Purpose	Perspective
Don't Forget Your Breakfast	to persuade	Possible response: Eating a healthful breakfast is important.
German Shepherds	to inform	Possible response: German shepherds are very useful dogs.

Harcourt

Fluency Builder

culture	years	would
chile	our	smell
mesquite	where	ground
barbecue	music	eight
accordion	know	neighbors
confetti	someone	their
	air	steaks

1. My name is / Roberto / and this is a story / about when I was eight years old.

2. My grandparents / traveled from a small town / where they know / all their neighbors.

3. Our Mexican culture / is important to us, / so we speak Spanish / at home.

4. My mother / always puts / an extra chile pepper / on the table / for my father.

5. My parents / told us / about the celebrations / they had in Mexico.

6. Someone / would play music / on an accordion.

7. The smell / of burning mesquite / filled the night air / as people / put steaks on the grill / to barbecue.

8. Only / the colorful confetti / on the ground / showed that / a celebration / had taken place.

Name _____

When I Was Eight

Circle and write the word that answers each riddle.

1. I have the vowel sound heard in *weigh*.
   I am a number. What am I?

   _____eight_____

   ten   (eight)   main

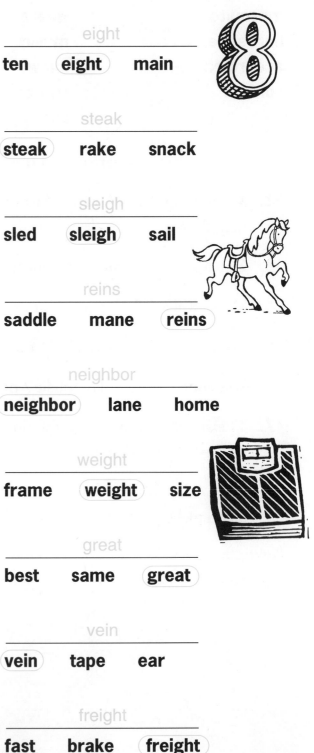

2. I have the vowel sound heard in *break*.
   I am a food. What am I?

   _____steak_____

   (steak)   rake   snack

3. I have the vowel sound heard in *neigh*.
   People ride in me on the snow. What am I? _____sleigh_____

   sled   (sleigh)   sail

4. I have the same vowel sound as in *vein*.
   You put me on a horse. What am I?

   _____reins_____

   saddle   mane   (reins)

5. I have the same vowel sound as in *weigh*.
   I live on your street. What am I?

   _____neighbor_____

   (neighbor)   lane   home

6. I have the same vowel sound as in *neigh*.
   You use a scale to find me. What am I?

   _____weight_____

   frame   (weight)   size

7. I have the vowel sound heard in *break*.
   I mean "very, very good." What am I?

   _____great_____

   best   same   (great)

8. I have the vowel sound heard in *rein*.
   I am inside your body. What am I?

   _____vein_____

   (vein)   tape   ear

9. I have the vowel sound heard in *weigh*.
   I am a kind of train. What am I?

   _____freight_____

   fast   brake   (freight)

Harcourt

When I Was Eight

Complete the sequence chart about "When I Was Eight." Write a sentence in each box. The first one has been done for you.

Event 1
(pages 198–199):

When Junior was eight years old, his grandparents came from Mexico to stay with his family for a month.

Event 2
(pages 200–201):

Possible response: On that visit, Junior's grandmother taught him and his sister how to make tortillas.

Event 3
(page 202):

Possible response: The family had a big celebration and ate the tortillas with chile, beans, and salsa.

Event 4
(pages 203–204):

Possible response: Junior's parents told stories about the fiestas they remembered from their childhood in Mexico.

Now use the information from the boxes to write a one-sentence summary of the selection.

Possible response: When his grandparents came to visit from Mexico, Junior enjoyed learning how to make tortillas and hearing stories about his parents' childhood in Mexico.

Sequence

Read the paragraph. Fill in the chart to show the sequence of events.

Every January my grandmother sends out invitations to our family reunion. On reunion day in June, we all meet at someone's house. Right away the cousins start a baseball game. Then we have a big picnic dinner. After dinner we name the oldest relative king or queen of the reunion. Before we leave, we decide where next year's reunion will be.

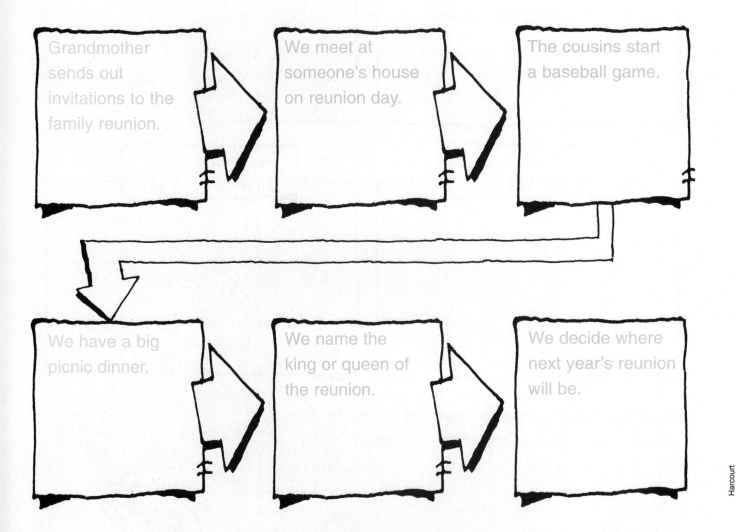

Grandmother sends out invitations to the family reunion.

We meet at someone's house on reunion day.

The cousins start a baseball game.

We have a big picnic dinner.

We name the king or queen of the reunion.

We decide where next year's reunion will be.

Harcourt

Name _____

Fluency Builder

abandoned	knew	firmly
profitable	work	breathless
beckons	over	comfortable
fares	could	quickly
rugged	were	hopeful
multicultural	used	beautiful
	make	
	out	

1. In the 1840s, / only rich people / could travel / to California by ship / as the fares were high.

2. James Marshall knew / there would be / few comforts there, / but he was rugged / and used to hard work.

3. Marshall was / firmly convinced / that the sawmill would / make his fortune.

4. Breathless, / he quickly lifted / the beautiful, / shiny stone / out of the water.

5. John Sutter was sure / the stones were gold, / but he wasn't comfortable / about the discovery.

6. The mill / was going to be / far more profitable / than a few small / gold stones.

7. Hopeful people / came from all over / with only one thing / in mind— / getting rich!

8. Sailors / abandoned their ships / and made their way / inland.

9. They made / California / a multicultural state / that today beckons travelers / from around the world.

Harcourt

The West Beckons

Read the story. Circle each word that ends with one of these suffixes: -ly, -ful, -able, -less.

Sadie is a playful puppy. When she thinks someone is having fun, she quickly joins in. Sadie is agreeable no matter what the game. Even if it is pointless, she will happily play.

One day a large truck slowly pulled up at the house next to Sadie's. Two cheerful movers got out of the truck and began to remove boxes. They were very careful with the first box.

Sadie thought it was a game, so she eagerly joined in. The movers were helpless. Sadie was unstoppable. Soon the lamp in the box was worthless.

Circle and write the word that best completes each sentence.

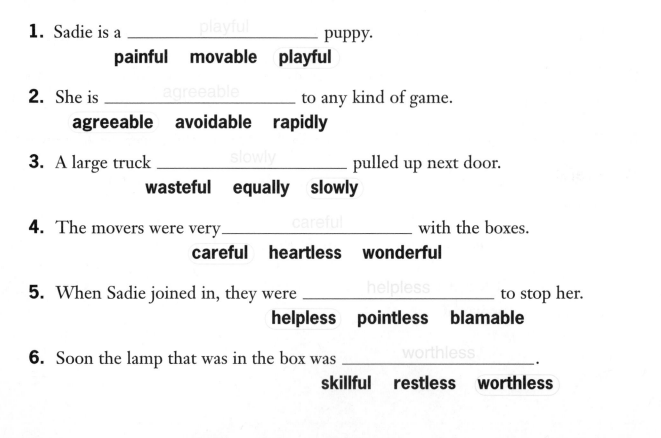

1. Sadie is a _____playful_____ puppy.
   painful   movable   playful

2. She is _____agreeable_____ to any kind of game.
   agreeable   avoidable   rapidly

3. A large truck _____slowly_____ pulled up next door.
   wasteful   equally   slowly

4. The movers were very_____careful_____ with the boxes.
   careful   heartless   wonderful

5. When Sadie joined in, they were _____helpless_____ to stop her.
   helpless   pointless   blamable

6. Soon the lamp that was in the box was _____worthless_____ .
   skillful   restless   worthless

Harcourt

The West Beckons

Write one or two sentences in each box below
to tell what you know about James Marshall
and the gold rush.

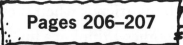

Pages 206–207

Why did James Marshall travel to California, and what did he hope to do once he got there?

Possible response: He traveled to California in order to find work. He hoped to make his fortune.

Page 208–209

What happened after Marshall discovered gold?

Possible response: People flocked to California hoping that they would find gold, too. Many of these people got in the way of the work at the sawmill, so Marshall sent them off to different parts of the unsettled territory. Some miners found gold there.

Pages 210–211

What effect did the gold rush have on California?

Possible response: It brought many people from around the world to live there. These people settled the land and made California a multicultural state that still beckons to travelers today.

Use the information above to write a one-sentence summary of the selection.

Possible response: James Marshall discovered gold in California and brought

about one of the largest gold rushes in North American history.

Harcourt

Fact and Opinion

Read the paragraph. In the chart below, write examples of fact and opinion statements from the paragraph. Possible response are given.

In my opinion, my little sister is a pest. Sometimes she follows me around for hours. She often asks to play with my friends when they come over. If I say "no," she cries. Usually I let her play. Sometimes I think it's fun to be with her. One time we pretended she was a baby bear and I was a daddy bear. I pretended to growl and snap at people who got near her. My sister said she loved that game. I thought it was fun, too.

	Characteristics	Examples from the Paragraph
Facts	Can be proven	Sometimes she follows me around for hours. She often asks to play with my friends when they come over. I pretended to growl and snap at people who got near her.
Opinions	Cannot be proven often use words such as "I think" or "I believe"	In my opinion, my little sister is a pest. Sometimes I think it's fun to be with her. I thought it was fun, too.

Harcourt

Fluency Builder

pioneer	that	tough
fertile	world	rough
harmony	days	though
arbor	named	through
possibilities	gold	
believed	find	
beautiful	found	
country	two	

1. The first Americans believed / that the mountain / kept their world / in harmony.

2. It took Zebulon Pike / and his crew / two tough days / to climb partway / up the mountain.

3. Even though / Pike never completed / the rough climb / to the top, / mapmakers named the mountain / Pikes Peak.

4. Stephen Long did make it / to the top, / and he saw a place / of endless possibilities.

5. When gold was discovered / on Pikes Peak, / the news spread / through busy cities / and shady country arbors.

6. Pioneers came / to Pikes Peak / hoping to find gold.

7. Rather than gold, / most people found / only a fertile landscape.

8. Katharine Lee Bates wrote / "America the Beautiful" / while looking out / from the top / of Pikes Peak.

Purple Mountain Majesty

Read the sentences and look at the picture. Follow the directions.

1. Ben smelled the baking dough. Add more lines to show the dough's aroma.
2. Ben brought three apples to the table. Add the apples to his bowl.
3. Ben thought about lunch. Draw in the bubble what he thought about.
4. Ben's wife had bought flowers. Add the flowers to the vase on the table.
5. Kim ate a doughnut. Draw the doughnut in her hand.
6. It is tough to play with a yo-yo while eating! Draw Kim's yo-yo.
7. There were enough plates for three people. Add the plates to the table.
8. The cat chased a mouse. Draw the mouse running through the room.
9. Two birds fought over some birdseed on the windowsill. Draw the birdseed.
10. The pinecone on the windowsill was rough on the outside. Draw the pinecone.

Now circle the words that have the *ough* letter pattern.

Name _____

Purple Mountain Majesty

Write one or two sentences in each box below to show what you have learned about the history of Pikes Peak.

Pages 214–215

Main Idea: Possible response: Hundreds of years ago, a great mountain at the edge of the plains played an important role in the lives of many Native American tribes. Then, in 1806, explorer Zebulon Pike made an attempt to climb the peak but failed.

Pages 216–217

Main Idea: Possible response: Stephen Long climbed the peak, but it was named Pikes Peak in honor of Zebulon Pike. Then gold was discovered and many people came to seek riches.

Pages 218–219

Main Idea: Possible response: Years later some people came to the mountain for the pure air. Katharine Lee Bates visited Pikes Peak and wrote the words to "America the Beautiful" while she was there.

Write a one-sentence summary of the selection.

Possible response: From ancient times through the end of the nineteenth

century, the mountain known as Pikes Peak was a place of hopes and

dreams.

Word Relationships

Read this paragraph.

Jenny had a nice bowl to sell. She decided to write an ad for the newspaper. By the time Jenny finished her ad, it was almost time for the newspaper office to close. She ran there so quickly that she came close to fainting. Jenny walked up the stairs to the office. The editor said he would add up the cost of an ad. It turned out that the price was very inexpensive. Jenny had enough money left over to bowl and go for pizza with her friends.

Read the list of word relationships in the column at the left. Then write examples from the paragraph in the column on the right.

How Words Are Related	Examples from the Paragraph
Synonyms: Words that have similar meanings	cost/price
Antonyms: Words that have opposite meanings	ran/walked
Homophones: Words that sound the same but have different spellings and meanings	ad/add
Homographs: Words that are spelled the same but have different meanings and pronunciations	close/close
Multiple-meaning word: Word that has more than one meaning	bowl

Harcourt

Name _____

Fluency Builder

bellowing	that	untamed
softhearted	for	impolite
ration	any	disagreeable
tragedy	use	impossible
fateful	when	nonsense
gadgets	wanted	unhappy
	who	
	from	

1. Pecos Bill was softhearted / toward the coyotes / that raised him.

2. Texas became / too calm / for the untamed spirit / of Pecos Bill.

3. Bill didn't use any gadgets / when he jumped on a rattler / of impossible size / and tied it into knots.

4. Bill was bellowing, / "Enough of this nonsense!"

5. Pecos Bill wanted cowboys / who were rough, / tough, / untamed, / impolite, / and disagreeable.

6. The wildcat nearly met / with tragedy / for trying to chew off / Bill's head.

7. Bill asked / for a ration / of grub / from the cowboys.

8. The unhappy cowpokes knew / that this was a fateful moment / for them.

Harcourt

An American Legend

Read the story, and circle all the words that have one of the following prefixes: *un-, re-, dis-, im-, non-,* or *pre-*.

Amaya and her family are at the airport. They are waiting to board their (nonstop) flight to New York. Amaya is (unhappy) because she forgot to pack a book to read. Her father (disappears) for a little while and comes back with a present for Amaya. She (unwraps) it and finds a book about (prehistoric) animals inside! Pleased, she hugs her father and begins to read.

"Would anyone like a drink?" asks Amaya's mom.

"I'd like some (nonfat) milk," says Amaya's father.

"I'd like a fruit drink," says Amaya.

Her mother goes to get the drinks. When she (reappears), she holds three cartons of milk. "I'm sorry, Amaya," she says. "It was (impossible) to find a fruit drink. But I bought you an apple to go with your milk."

"Thank you, Mom!" says Amaya.

Now write the word with a prefix from above that best completes each sentence. Use each word only once.

1. It is _____impossible_____ for Amaya's mom to find a fruit drink.

2. When Amaya _____unwraps_____ her present, she finds a book inside.

3. A _____nonstop_____ flight does not stop anywhere along the way.

4. Amaya is _____unhappy_____ because she forgot a book for her trip.

5. She likes to read about _____prehistoric_____ animals.

6. Amaya's dad likes _____nonfat_____ milk.

7. Amaya's mom _____reappears_____ after being away for a short time.

8. Amaya's unhappiness _____disappears_____ when she finds the book.

An American Legend

Complete the chart about "An American Legend." Write a sentence or two in each box. The first has been done for you.

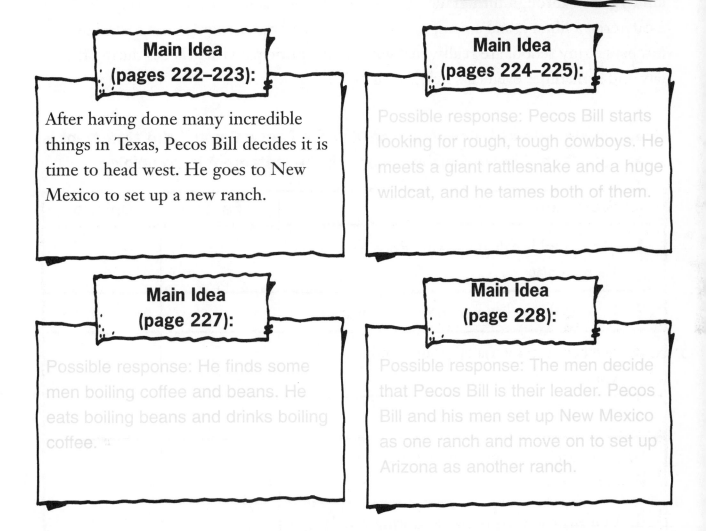

Main Idea (pages 222–223):

After having done many incredible things in Texas, Pecos Bill decides it is time to head west. He goes to New Mexico to set up a new ranch.

Main Idea (pages 224–225):

Possible response: Pecos Bill starts looking for rough, tough cowboys. He meets a giant rattlesnake and a huge wildcat, and he tames both of them.

Main Idea (page 227):

Possible response: He finds some men boiling coffee and beans. He eats boiling beans and drinks boiling coffee.

Main Idea (page 228):

Possible response: The men decide that Pecos Bill is their leader. Pecos Bill and his men set up New Mexico as one ranch and move on to set up Arizona as another ranch.

Now use the information from the boxes above to write a one-sentence summary of the selection.

Possible response: The legendary Pecos Bill leaves Texas, tames a giant rattlesnake and a huge wildcat, and finds men who help him set up New Mexico and Arizona as ranches.

Fact and Opinion

Read this paragraph. Think about which statements are fact and which are opinion.

My school is called Eleanor Roosevelt Elementary. It has classrooms for kindergarten through fifth grade. E. R. is the greatest school in the district! We have a cafeteria, a library, and a computer room. The computer room is the best. The teachers at my school are really, really nice. Our principal visits classes during the day and sometimes even eats lunch with us.

Read the statements below. Mark an *X* in the Fact column if the statement is a fact. Mark an *X* in the Opinion column if the statement is an opinion.

Statement	Fact	Opinion
1. My school is called Eleanor Roosevelt Elementary.	X	
2. E. R. is the greatest school in the district!		X
3. We have a cafeteria, a library, and a computer room.	X	
4. The computer room is the best.		X
5. The teachers at my school are really, really nice.		X
6. Our principal visits classes during the day and sometimes even eats lunch with us.	X	

Harcourt

Fluency Builder

carnivorous	bat	notion
boggiest	into	concentration
chemicals	sometimes	solution
dissolve	have	direction
accidentally	days	motion
fertilizer	eyes	
victim	help	
	down	

1. Brown Bat heads / in the direction / of the boggiest marshes / to hunt.

2. Brown Bat uses / a flipping motion / to toss mosquitoes / into his mouth.

3. Fertilizers / and chemicals / are sometimes stored / in garden sheds.

4. The bolas spider / uses great skill / and concentration / to catch moths.

5. The moths have / no notion / that they / are being watched.

6. There are days / when a bolas spider / accidentally misses with his bolas.

7. The bolas spider injects a solution / to dissolve his bug roll-up.

8. The praying mantis has five eyes / that help him watch / for victims.

9. All of these carnivorous creatures / help keep down / the insect population.

Bug Catchers

Mark the letter in front of the sentence that tells about the picture.

1 **A** It is the end of January.
B It is time for summer vacation.
C It is time for winter hibernation.
D This is a new invention.

2 **A** Boris wants to go to the seashore.
B Boris tells how to add fractions.
C Boris will take some of his possessions.
D Boris talks about possible destinations.

3 **A** Stella does not like road construction.
B Stella thinks there is too much pollution.
C Stella likes this situation very much.
D Stella says there is a lot of relaxation.

4 **A** Boris has a great solution.
B Boris will go to the city alone.
C Boris ends the conversation.
D Boris tries long division.

5 **A** He will watch whale migration.
B He is watching television.
C He suggests jungle exploration.
D He suggests making a donation.

6 **A** They sail away on their vacation.
B They go to the train station.
C They fly to their destination.
D They go into hibernation.

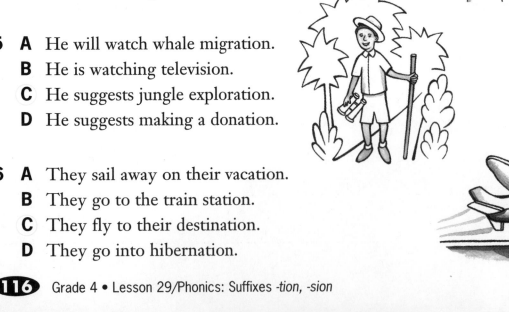

Bug Catchers

**Write one or two sentences in each box
to show how different creatures catch bugs.**

Pages 230–231

How do brown bats catch bugs? Possible response: They hunt in boggy marshes for mosquitoes. They find their prey by screeching, and when the sound bounces back, they can tell the location of the mosquito.

Pages 232–233

How do bolas spiders catch bugs? Possible response: Bolas spiders make a silky thread with a sticky blob at one end to toss at their prey.

Pages 234–236

How do praying mantises catch bugs? Praying mantises wait and watch for victims, and when one gets close, they catch it by snapping shut their powerful legs.

**Use the information above to write a one-sentence summary of
the selection.**

Possible response: Many creatures eat bugs, and some bug catchers have

amazing ways of snagging their prey.

Harcourt

Word Relationships

Read this paragraph.

The day was hot, although it had been cool this morning. I used my hat to fan my face. At last, it was my turn up at bat. I watched the pitcher turn toward me. He threw the ball as I raised my bat. The ball whizzed through the air. Crack! I hit the ball as hard as I could. Every fan cheered and screamed. We would win the game!

Read the list of word relationships in the column on the left. Write sentences from the paragraph that are examples in the column on the right.

How Words Are Related	Examples from the Paragraph
Synonyms	Every fan <u>cheered</u> and <u>screamed.</u>
Antonyms	The day was <u>hot</u>, although it had been <u>cool</u> this morning.
Homophones	He <u>threw</u> the ball and I raised my bat. The ball whizzed <u>through</u> the air.
Multiple-meaning words	I used my hat to <u>fan</u> my face. Every <u>fan</u> cheered.

Harcourt

Fluency Builder

transformed	new	classmates
investigate	across	soccer
enthusiastically	and	writing
decor	may	baseball
apparently	into	interrupted
corridor	get	advantages
		future

1. Paul is writing / to his future classmate / to investigate / what his new school / will be like.

2. Apparently / the moose Paul came across / was not familiar / with humans.

3. The decor / of Paul's classroom / and corridor / is very similar / to Ricardo's classroom.

4. Ricardo may be sent / to the states / and transformed / into a Californian.

5. Ricardo enthusiastically / tells Paul / about the Spanish World Cup / soccer team.

6. Paul will need / to teach Ricardo / about baseball.

7. Air Force kids / get their plans interrupted / a lot.

8. Being an Air Force kid / has its advantages.

Name _____

Air Force Kids

Circle and write the word that makes the sentence tell about the picture.

1. Wilbur and Judy Morris live in a big

   _____ city _____ .

   (city) foundry parlor

2. From time to time they enjoy camping

   in the _____ wilderness _____ .

   seashore (wilderness) cinema

3. First, they go to the _____ market _____

   to get supplies. (market) palace program

4. They put their _____ equipment _____ in backpacks.

   finches (equipment) bubbles

5. They hike up a _____ gentle _____

   corner (gentle) pinch

   slope for several hours.

6. They pass through a meadow full of

   colorful _____ flowers _____ .

   flashes (flowers) starlings

7. They find a _____ perfect _____

   celebrate forward (perfect)

   place to make their camp.

Now draw a line between the syllables of each word you wrote.

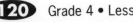

Air Force Kids

Write one or two sentences in each box to tell what you learned about Ricardo and Paul in "Air Force Kids."

Pages 238–239

What did you learn about where the characters live? Possible response: Ricardo lives in Spain, where he has seen animals in a nearby village. Paul lives in Alaska, where he can sometimes see a moose.

Pages 240–241

What else did you learn about each character? Possible response: Ricardo has lived in Germany, Turkey, and Spain, and he plays soccer. Paul has never been outside the U.S., and he goes snowshoeing in the wintertime.

Pages 242–243

What does Ricardo find out in these pages? Possible response: First he learns that he'll be moving to California soon, and he's worried he'll go before Paul gets there. Then he finds out he won't move for a year, so he'll get to meet Paul and go with him to a soccer match.

Use the information above to write a one-sentence summary of the selection.

Possible response: Although pen pals Paul and Ricardo live far away from each other, they are both Air Force kids and they can't wait to meet each other when Paul's family moves to Spain.

Author's Purpose

Read the paragraph and think about the author's purpose. Then fill in the chart below. List the details that helped you determine the author's purpose.

Tarantulas are members of the spider family. Tarantulas have eight legs. Their legs and bodies are covered in hair. Tarantulas do not spin webs. They capture their prey by chasing it. Tarantulas feed mainly on insects, but they have been known to eat small frogs, toads, and mice. The bite of the tarantula is not dangerous to humans, but many people are afraid of them.

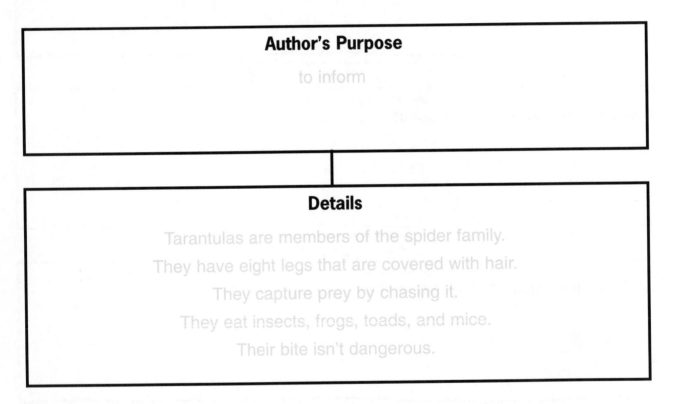

Author's Purpose
to inform

Details
Tarantulas are members of the spider family.
They have eight legs that are covered with hair.
They capture prey by chasing it.
They eat insects, frogs, toads, and mice.
Their bite isn't dangerous.

Do you think the author thinks that tarantulas are interesting, boring, or dangerous? Why?

_____

_____

_____

Harcourt